Modelling the SOUTHERN

Volume 1: Ideas and Inspiration

Jeremy English

Noodle *N.B.* Books

© Jeremy English and Noodle Books 2012

ISBN 978-1-906419-75-2

First published in 2012 by Kevin Robertson
under the **NOODLE BOOKS** imprint
PO Box 279
Corhampton
SOUTHAMPTON
SO32 3ZX

www.noodlebooks.co.uk

Printed in England by The Information Press.

Front cover - *Locomotive detailing: pull-push fitted 'M7' No 30021 on station pilot duties at Salisbury on 28 April 1962. Usually the short-frame non-fitted M7s were used on such duties, the p/p ones being reserved, not surprisingly, for p/p work. Notice the engine head-lamps of different type as well as the spare tail-lamp carried on the front buffer beam. The latter would not be needed if operating solely within station limits, nor are the usual headcode discs required. Ignore the signal box in the background!*

Photo: Roger Holmes 2210

Title page - *The archetypical 'Brighton' goods: single dome 'C2X' No. 32541 with the pick-up goods at Cranleigh on the line between Guildford and Christ's Hospital. The two headcode discs confirm the route, being used for all trains between Guildford and Horsham. Goods workings are featured in this volume: the Southern did have goods trains (and plenty of them)!*

Rear cover - *Ian Wright's delightful model of one of the most eccentric locomotives inherited by the Southern - Dugald Drummond's first express engine for the LSWR - stands at the down starter at the model Romsey station with what was its most common type of working in its latter days, a parcels train. No. E720 was the sole example of its class, T7, and had two pairs of uncoupled driving wheels, being known as a 'Double-single' (there were 5 more, of class E10, with smaller boilers). A ready-to-run model of this oddity is unlikely to be produced, but we'll be looking at kits for such prototypes in Volume 2.*

Opposite - *Graham 'Muz' Muspratt has carved out a niche for himself with his magnificent revocation of the pivot of the West of England line, Salisbury. His 'Fisherton Sarum' shed scene is set on the cusp of Nationalisation, with locomotives sporting the brilliant Bulleid Malachite Green livery. Here one of the two malachite liveried N Class Locomotives, no. 1854, simmers outside the front of the LSWR Style shed at Fisherton Sarum. See more in Chapter 9.*

Photo: courtesy of Chris Nevard and Hornby Magazine

Modelling the Southern

Where it all began for me. New Milton station is one of three more-or-less identical stations on the Bournemouth Direct line from Lymington Junction to Christchurch through the New Forest. I lived there from infancy until age 18 and my passion for railways was nurtured by the sight of Bulleid Pacifics thundering through or slipping madly if they had to restart for any reason. The station design was more or less an LSWR standard in the late Victorian age.
Below *is Douglas Smith's magnificent recreation of one, or, rather, all of these stations, which he has named Swaynton. There's a feature on Swaynton at the end of the book. Philip Hall, courtesy of Wild Swan Publications Ltd.*

Introduction

W hat I am trying to describe in this little tome is what might be called the 'Essence of Southern' because I believe that surely is what one is trying to achieve when 'Modelling the Southern'. I was going to sub-title it 'Getting it Right' but felt that was holding myself hostage to fortune, although that does describe the intention; so it's 'Ideas and Inspiration'. All I can say, like the author of a book of fiction (which this isn't), is "any mistakes are mine and mine alone".

Right here at the start I must 'set out my stall'. I am talking here about 4mm scale models, usually designed to run on 16.5mm gauge track, otherwise known as 00 gauge. I don't want to stir up all the emotions that use of the 'incorrect' gauge causes, so, to clear the air at the outset, throughout this book I shall refer simply to 4mm scale and encompass the various Finescale 00, EM gauge and P4/S4 standards within that term. 2mm scale, (N gauge), and 7mm (0 gauge), will also be mentioned, but since 4mm scale represents about 85% of the market, it will predominate. Of course, the prototype descriptions are equally relevant to any model scale. I am going to assume that the reader is familiar with general railway terms and titles such as BR, CME, Mk1, Standard, wagon, stock and signal as well as common modelling terms such as scratch-building, ready-to-run, kits, trackwork and so on. This is not a book covering basic railway facts or modelling techniques, those have been written by modellers with far greater abilities and experience than I.

For many years the Southern Railway was the poor relation in respect of models by the principal model railway manufacturers. However, Hornby effectively changed all that - and how enthusiastic modellers viewed it - when it launched a brand new model of one of the most famous preserved steam locomotives, 'Clan Line', at the beginning of the 21st Century.

The specification of the model was so different to what had gone before that it was instantly catapulted to the very top of the list of quality ready-to-run models and the Hornby brand was changed forever. In fact 'Clan Line' was just one of three models offered of members of the renowned 'Merchant Navy' class designed by Oliver Bulleid and rebuilt under the auspices of Ron Jarvis: just what Southern modellers had despaired ever of seeing.

To go with these 'Rebuilt Merchant Navies' Hornby produced some brand-new models of Pullman coaches and offered them in a set accurately portraying the famous 'Bournemouth Belle'. These coaches were equally ahead of the pack, being scale models in almost all respects, fitted with separate details such as ventilators and footsteps, which had traditionally been part of the basic body mouldings of previous coach models. There was even an "add-on pack" of differently-numbered coaches to make a six-coach train, and some "loose" models in the normal coaching range, which enabled a complete train to be made up - from a manufacturer which had previously issued just one number or name for each locomotive or coach and produced it over a period of many years! Modellers snapped them up.

However, it was the mere fact that it was *Hornby* that had created a 'proper' scale model that caused a sensation. The 'Merchant Navies' were the classic 'glamour' type that Hornby had always indulged in as part of its 'toy train' image and its release wasn't actually the first good Southern model. That accolade goes to Bachmann, who released their first 'Blue Riband' product, a Maunsell N class mogul, in 1998. The success of these two locomotive types showed that there was a pent up demand for good Southern models. Hornby responded to this with a series of Southern prototypes which would allow a fairly representative Southern locomotive fleet to be built up, as well as a revamp of most of the previous 'glamour' models of locomotives of the other railways (because most of us like to find an excuse to run locomotives from the 'other' railways on even the most staunchly Southern layout!). Within a decade, most of the Hornby line-up was of scale models rather than toys. Bachmann underlined this with models of most of the Standard steam types which worked on the Southern in BR days.

Whilst researching this book I came across far more material than is possible to include in one book, so this has now become the first part of a short series. Herein I will concentrate on what is available 'ready to run'. Kits etc. will appear in later volumes.

The other major parameter is the time span: just so you know, this work covers the period from 1st January 1923 to 9th July 1967, from the inception of the Southern Railway to the last day of steam on British Railways Southern Region, the day when the Southern's inheritance was finally subsumed within the Corporate era. The term 'Southern' hereafter refers to that 44½ year period. And, finally, where the modeller is referred to as 'he' please understand that this term is not intended to be exclusive but is used as shorthand to cover members of both genders rather than to write 'he or she' many times over.

Obviously, this isn't a definitive work: such a massive subject as the Southern could only be done justice in an encyclopaedia. It is, rather, an attempt to describe the unique features of the Southern in order to show what to incorporate so that a Southern model shouts out its provenance for those who are 'modelling the Southern'.

Jeremy English

1 Why model the Southern?

The first thing a modeller has to consider is quite what kind of model railway he wants to achieve. The second is *what* he will be *able* to achieve - often a very different thing!

Most modellers are principally constrained by a lack of space. This restricts the ability to model an accurate scale replica of most main line stations and even many branch line ones. Normally, only club layouts can produce scale replicas, and even these have to incorporate 'scenic breaks' and curves which didn't happen on the prototype. However, the Southern had plenty of small-scale branches and suburban lines which can be reproduced, with a few alterations, to give the 'essence' which we are pursuing here. It also *failed* to serve many places which, in the modeller's parallel universe, can be used as the site of fictional models which can display all the characteristics of a 'real' Southern railway model. This latter approach is by far the most popular one, adopted by most modellers, as it allows the enthusiast to observe the whole railway picture and to choose those parts which appeal to him. He can then weld them together to create his own preferred 'legend' and overall picture. That requires a certain amount of knowledge and observation to ensure that the chosen features don't clash, so that those who think they know it all can't pick out anything in their nit-picking way. That's what I'm trying to help you avoid here - let's not give them anything to get their teeth into!

There is one over-riding factor that transcends everything you do on a model railway - 'Rule Number One'. That states 'It's my railway and I can do whatever I want on it' (sometimes it's referred to as the 'Modeller's Licence'). If what I say is anathema to you, you are free to ignore it! You may want to run named Pacifics on one-coach trains or goods engines on expresses or LNER B1s in southern Hampshire - and you are free to do so, it's your railway. But then, all those things happened anyway, a characteristic known as the 'prototype for everything' rule. So that's where we're going to start, by looking at the prototype. You'll probably find that most things you want to do were done on the real Southern anyway.

"You may want to run named Pacifics on one-coach trains or goods engines on expresses or LNER B1s in southern Hampshire - and you are free to do so, it's your railway."

Wednesday 6 May 1959 found ER 'B1' No. 61119 storming through Botley (in southern Hampshire) on the 6.03 pm special working from Portsmouth Harbour to Leytonstone. The service, an excursion, had left London at 8.35 am the same morning booked as having '10 L.M. coaches' - someone got that a bit wrong at least. Half the fun of planning the model is finding out things like this, finding a photograph to confirm it to others can often be more difficult. Hence the beauty and variety of the hobby, there is so much to indulge in.

Ron Roberts

Why model the Southern?

Why indeed? Historically, from the early days of modelling, the Southern was regarded primarily as only a suitable prototype for a small country branch terminus. This may have been because there were few available models of Southern prototypes meaning the modeller had to scratch build the majority of the stock and scenery, and smaller subjects were simpler to do. It may also have had its roots in the fact that there were evidently fewer railway enthusiasts in the South of the United Kingdom than further North: the culture of railway enthusiasm has always appeared to be more intense in industrial cities than rural or commuter country, and the culture of the South was never quite so indulgent of such enthusiasm. Further, it may be that, traditionally, it was the steam locomotive which attracted the most interest, and the Southern was perceived as an electric, suburban railway, and thus of little interest.

However, things have changed.

It seems that the peak of railway enthusiasm was reached with the post-WW2 'baby boomer' generation and as they have grown to maturity they have become both more secure in their enjoyment of the hobby and have the time and space to indulge that hobby, whilst Society has become more tolerant of hobbies generally. Many of those in the South, who had little incentive to admit to an enthusiasm in their youth, are now avid modellers and the railway they remember is the Southern! And that, after all, is the first, and basic reason, for 'modelling the Southern'.

A further reason is that, despite the "electric railway"

perception, the Southern had what was perhaps the widest spread of pre-grouping locomotives surviving into Nationalisation - precisely *because* the Southern's main priority was electrification. Thus LSWR T9 'Greyhounds' and B4 dock shunters, a wide variety of SER and LCDR 4-4-0s and a myriad of Brighton tanks were still to be seen at work well into the 1950s, not to mention the famous Beattie Well Tanks, Terriers, and Adams Radials which were still in service in the early 1960s. A further Southern anomaly was the self-contained Isle of Wight system which had complete Edwardian trains running into the mid-1960s.

Locomotives are the primary interest of many (most?) enthusiasts and the Southern's use of steam even on express trains until the late 1960s is a strong incentive to model it. There was only one class of main line diesel built by BR specifically for Southern use (the BRCW type 3, later class 33) but there were also the unique Electro-Diesels and, in the 1950s, the Southern Region actually had *all* of BR's main line diesels (bar one, the 'Fell') working on it. It also had pure electric locomotives and for a short time, the most controversial British locomotive ever, the (in)famous Bulleid 'Leader'. As they've grown older, Southern enthusiasts have grown to appreciate this and know that, for those modellers who want a variety of motive power, the Southern had it in abundance.

Not only did the Southern have a great variety of motive power, but it had a great variety of trains, from intensive main line suburban commuter trains and expresses to rural and cross-country branch line services. The lines themselves were incredibly varied, it had eight track main lines, such as Waterloo to Clapham Jct and

The quintessential Southern view: Bulleid Pacifics in both their forms stand at the country end of Waterloo in the 1960s. 'Bodmin', in modified form, shows a tail lamp as the train to which it is attached has probably been worked into the terminus Alongside is an 'original' - the descriptions have caused much dissent in the enthusiast community - Fighter Command', unique in the class as it boasted a Giesl ejector from 1962 onwards

London Bridge to New Cross, fierce climbs, like Folkestone Harbour or Ilfracombe (both of which *really* made locomotives bark) and charismatic branches such as the Lyme Regis, Hayling, and Kent & East Sussex, each with its own enormous individual character.

Whereas once upon a time it was necessary to scratch or kit-build most of the required stock for a Southern model, today, if you just want to open boxes and get on with running your trains, the Southern has a great amount to offer. This means it takes far less time to assemble the loco fleet and to construct the layout, so you can have a bigger fleet and a bigger layout or spend more time in getting the details right. In 4mm scale/00 gauge (just 4mm scale from hereon) the "new" Hornby has produced a well balanced range of Southern prototypes with its three types of Bulleid Pacific, "King Arthurs", "Schools", Drummond M7s and T9s, and the Bulleid Q1 "Charlies", all of which were to be seen at work across the Southern at some time in their careers. Bachmann can add to this line-up with its N moguls and Wainwright C class, and its splendid range of BR Standard types, most of which worked on the Southern in BR(SR) days. Special commissions by traders, such as Kernow with their Beattie Well Tank and 02 models, are rounding this out. Both of the large companies provide Southern carriages to go with them, and freight wagons are pretty much universal in application so there is almost everything one could want available off the shelf. So that's what we're going to concentrate on in this book.

Even railway infrastructure is being addressed: some buildings and scenic accessories are available "ready to plant", including Southern classics such as signal boxes, footbridges, station buildings and goods facilities. Recently too the LBSCR style of building as seen on the Bluebell line but which style also featured on the Chichester - Midhurst route. Small parts such as yard lamps, water cranes, station name boards and fencing are available from specialist suppliers and manufacturers.

For the individualist there are still plenty of kits available for lesser-known and more obscure prototypes, whether of locomotives or rolling stock, in particular there are complete kits or simply replacement sides to create many of the characteristic carriages which have not, and probably never will be, addressed by the ready-to-run manufacturers. Of course, buildings and signals may still be few and far between, but the availability of so many other Southern models gives the modeller more time to spend on creating the "missing" items and thus still give his layout that air of individuality. We'll cover some of those here but go into them in more detail in a subsequent volume, the intention being to slowly move from what can be bought off the shelf towards what one can do, or make, for oneself. What this isn't, is a blow-by-blow account of building a model or a model railway: it seeks to provide ideas and inspiration and to help the modeller to answer the question 'why model the Southern?'.

There's a common misconception that the Southern didn't run double-headers. It did, but not often. Here's a pair of Pacifics, climbing up from Ilfracombe on the notorious 1 in 36 to the summit at Morthoe. This double-track branch saw much variety of motive power in the summer, even boasting Great Western locomotives and banking turns.

This is what the Southern was all about, a mix of steam and electric. For many years the only ready to run EMUs available were the early Tri-ang suburban set or Hornby-Dublo EPB, both loosely based on the prototype. But times have moved on and apart from a plethora of excellent kits there is the promise of additional accurate units to come. Here at Farnham steam and electric combine, the latter in the form of the electric car sheds in the background and steam with the Drummond '700' (a personal favourite - and a hot tip for r-t-r production) lifting a rake of loco-hauled ex-LSWR Ironclad coaches out of what were the sand-pit sidings. The point for the modeller is: how often do we see a layout where there is such an obvious change in levels? Railways were not always flat and gradient variation can have such visual impact. Just a thought of course…..!

Courtesy Carole Griffiths

Left - Another suggestion, Lymington. The trainshed at Lymington Town would make for something rather different. Notice also the catchpoint and the position of its associated ground-signal, all too often both are lacking. The smoke effect might be more difficult to achieve and is not recommended to be attempted indoors.

Lymington, of course, had two stations, the Pier being situated just a short way beyond Town. An enterprising modeller or Group might use this as the basis of a very interesting layout, and boat modellers could find a niche here too! Trains weren't confined to pull-push, as the line had up to five through trains to Waterloo on Summer Saturdays. Maunsell Q class 0-6-0s were favourites on these and the pick-up goods and in earlier times even T9s would occasionally venture along the branch.

2 Southern Constituents and Character

"What did 'The Southern' do?" "What was the make-up of the Southern?" "How was it structured?" and "What made it so special?" are all pertinent questions to be asked and answered before commencing a model.

Carrying passengers was the raison d'être of the Southern. Whilst its contemporaries were built on a base of goods (or freight) traffic, the Southern was built on passengers. Each of its three main constituent companies served seaports, each ran to popular holiday destinations and each had major suburban systems. Those three constituents were;

> The London and South Western Railway
> (LSWR or "the South Western")
> The London, Brighton and South Coast Railway
> (LBSCR or "the Brighton")
> The South Eastern and Chatham Railway
> (SECR - it had no common nickname!)

The LSWR had a main line from London Waterloo to Southampton and Bournemouth eventually arriving at Weymouth, another to Portsmouth and finally the famous West of England main line through Salisbury and Yeovil to Exeter. It also had an extensive suburban system in the south-west part of London, and numerous branches throughout Wessex. And then there was the iconic "Withered Arm" beyond Exeter, serving North Devon and Cornwall and the basis for proportionately more Southern models than any other part of the system. Its main port was Southampton, which it had developed into the principal Trans-Atlantic and Colonial port for the entire country. Of all the Southern constituents, the LSWR was the nearest to a national company with its many trains to northern cities and cross-country destinations. Its part ownership of the legendary Somerset & Dorset Joint Railway even gives the modeller the opportunity to justify locomotives and stock from the LMS on a Southern layout. The Southern assumed responsibility for the infrastructure and rolling stock of the S&D from 1930, for the line in general from

Nationalisation in 1948 and for locomotives from 1950 to 1958.

The LBSCR had a main line from London Victoria and London Bridge to Brighton. It lived up to the second part of its name with lines that ran along the South Coast from Brighton to Portsmouth and to Eastbourne and Hastings. The Sussex countryside was served by numerous secondary main lines and branches, many of them interconnecting with one another. It, too, had an extensive suburban system in London, encompassing the southern dormitory towns and suburbs. Its principal seaport was Newhaven, serving the Cross-Channel traffic to Normandy. Perceived by many as having been electrified early in Southern days and thus written off as a suitable subject for modelling, it had a large non-electrified system in East Sussex with tremendous character right to the end of steam and beyond, part of which was the foundation of the great British railway preservation movement in the shape of the famous 'Bluebell Railway'.

The SECR was, strictly speaking, two railway companies. The title was an abbreviation of the South Eastern and Chatham Companies Joint Management Committee, created in 1899 to work the railway assets of the South Eastern Railway and the London, Chatham and Dover Railway, two companies which had fought for control over the Kent countryside in the 19th Century, virtually bankrupting both of them. The legacy was two main lines to Dover, and two lines and stations in every town of any significance throughout "The Garden of England". During their independent existence, the two companies had fought hard over the "Continental" traffic (it was always "The Continent", not Europe, in steam days), and from the Thames southwards in the south-eastern part of London the two companies had built a massive suburban network, again frequently duplicating services from a myriad of London termini. The Cinque Port of Dover and the Harbours at Ramsgate and Folkestone all had facilities owned and served by these lines, as did a number of smaller ports and harbours.

Opposite - No prizes for guessing the line, the Somerset & Dorset of course, and no excuse needed for its inclusion. The location is Midford, a down train seen behind an LMS (ex Midland) 2P No. 655 sometime in the 1930s. Like the SECR, the Midland had followed a practice of small locomotives for many years. Then, like the Southern, the LMS as successor to the Midland reversed that policy completely. A simple scene of the type all too often discounted when considering a prototype, but think again, what a wonderful subject for a model, the curving main line, the gradient, and the solitary goods siding. Signalling included the famous 'backing signal' on top of the short tunnel here - S&DJR signalling was supplied by the LSWR and later the Southern. If your interest is big engines, and lots of them, then of course perhaps consider modelling a loco depot. Similarly your wishes may lean towards a through station, branch line - whatever. But here, if scenery and landscaping is your penchant then there is the opportunity to excel. Less is often more and done well this could be a real show-stopper.

Horstead Keynes around the time of opening in 1885 (the similar Sheffield Park is available as a model from Bachman), and a bastion of steam until the end, seeing many LBSCR locomotives and rolling stock into the 1950s. Station architectural styles varied as much over decades as well as companies. In this respect the Southern was no different to other railways, some lines, and especially their infrastructure, built to a 'standard' format, whilst others were promoted as a 'private' venture where the design of building used would have been unique to that line - or even that location. Then when absorbed into the Southern, the railway inherited a true variety of structures.

For modellers, its use of 4-4-0s on heavy expresses right to the end of the 1950s and the same engines on many branches give the SECR a very special flavour. The competing lines to most towns mean that short trains can be prototypically correct on almost any working and through trains to London can be justified without further question.

It might be said that the Southern had three-and-a-half main constituents as it had inherited a half share in the Somerset & Dorset Joint Railway, which ran from Broadstone on the 'Old Road' to Bath on the former Midland Railway. The 'Joint' in its name didn't mean it was run by Hippies, but indicated its 50% ownership by the Southern and LMS, which they received at Grouping from the LSWR and Midland. It was a hugely charismatic line, with its main line split into single and double track parts, seemingly at random. The LSWR, and thus Southern, provided its infrastructure and signalling so it *looked* like a Southern line, until the locomotives appeared. They were provided by the Midland/LMS and thus 2Ps, 4Fs, Black 5s and Johnson 3Fs ran to Poole and Bournemouth West. At nationalisation the line effectively became wholly

Southern as it fell into the Southern Region, which started to provide its own locomotives from 1950. Thus Bulleids, T9s and so on appeared along with many LMS survivors until the evil (Great) Western Region took it over in 1958, and proceeded to make sure it would be closed. Modellers love it, and so do I, so from hereon I intend to treat it as an integral part of the Southern!

In general, the Southern split its organisation into administrative areas based on the original constituent companies' lines, and these were variously known as Sections or Divisions, the title change coming after Nationalisation but not immediately. Herein I shall refer to the SR period areas as Sections and the BR period ones as Divisions, although the actual routes sometimes fell into different areas as time passed. Like BR, the Southern was forever changing how it described its working arrangements! So, from now on the old SECR lines are the Eastern Section or Eastern Division, the LBSCR ones the Central and the LSWR ones the Western. (I could go on a bit here, as the ex-LSWR lines in the Western Section had a London Division, Central Division and a Western Division as well and the term District was also used at some periods! I'm sure you get the general idea, fortunately the exact terms have little relevance to modelling).

In addition to its three main constituents the Southern incorporated a number of much smaller undertakings, notably three separate railways on the little Isle of Wight, the Isle of Wight Railway (IWR), the Isle of Wight Central Railway (IWCR) and the Freshwater and Yarmouth Railway (FYR). In South Devon it acquired the Plymouth, Devonport and South Western Junction Railway (PDSWR), a nominally independent company set up to build a railway from Tavistock into Plymouth and a branch line across into Cornwall near Callington. A number of models have featured the Isle of Wight lines, Ventnor (either station!) in particular being an almost perfect prototype to be built to scale, whilst the PDSWJR's little covered terminus near Callington would make a very unusual and attractive model.

All the railways of the Southern had strategic naval purposes, as Plymouth, Portsmouth and Chatham were the principal Royal Navy ports to protect the country from possible Continental predators. The naval authorities had been very influential in their support of the construction of the railways which were to become the Southern Railway system. They were also in the front line during both World Wars, serving a vital function in provisioning the country's armies fighting on the Continent and supporting the RAF which had its principal fighter airfields in Southern territory. The Army had bases across the South, many of which were served by branch lines off the Southern and included the well-known Longmoor Military Railway, on which immaculate locomotives of all sizes worked trains formed of extremely old carriage stock on what might be the only example of that classic 'non-prototypical' form of layout - the continuous run, or 'roundy-roundy' layout - another example of a Southern-related railway that proves the cynics wrong! (Don't forget either that some of the Southern electric services were operated along similar, although not identical, principals.)

With little industry, the South of England's principal economy outside the cities has been agricultural. Thus the Southern's goods traffic reflected this, the railway carrying market produce in fast goods trains to the metropolis. Strawberries, milk, apples, hops, bananas and everything else that grows in the ground or above

Half a century on and Southern architectural design was very much into the 'art-deco', sometimes referred to as the 'Odeon' style. Seen here at the rebuilt Surbiton, the use of concrete is very much to the fore.

it, plus perishable imported food, were carried in the Southern's trains, not forgetting livestock. The seaports also provided much traffic, both inward and outward, as the ports in the South of England gave the quickest routes both to the Continent and the British Empire. The only features often associated with railways that were in short supply or missing on the Southern system were industrial mills and collieries, although, as always, there were plenty of exceptions; Kent boasted a coalfield, the S&D a number of collieries and there were many breweries and warehouses as well as industrial plants across the system. It was just that these developed later and came about because of the railway, rather than the other way round, as had happened 'oop north'.

Another difference to those northern railways was the frequency of the (passenger) services the Southern ran. The LSWR had pioneered the concept of 'clock-face' timings for departures from its principal stations, notably Waterloo, from where trains to the West of England left on the hour and those to the Bournemouth line left on the half hour: its suburban electric trains ran to similar clock-face timings from the many suburban stations as they were in competition with the trams and timetables were things commuters had little interest in. Southern services to most of its lines were frequent, if not hourly, through the day; it wasn't just a case of one or two trains a day as occurred on some of the more remote areas served by the 'other' railways.

With the frequency of trains came more elaborate station facilities as each station served more passengers, although there were plenty of rather basic stations on the rural lines. Each of the constituent companies had its own particular style, those styles of course varying according to the era in which they were built. Goods facilities changed over the years as well, but there were only a very few locations where there were massive marshalling yards, even these paling into the background by comparison with the industrial yards of the non-Southern railways. The LSWR had also pioneered the use of concrete from its Exmouth Junction works for virtually every structure on the railway, a policy which the Southern expanded to cover all of its empire, creating a very distinctive style which was commonly associated with its 'Southern Electric' image but which was actually to be seen almost everywhere. 'Concrete' features on a model railway help establish its Southern provenance even before a train hoves into view.

But whilst the Railway Clearing House had set standards to allow interchange of 'common-user' stock across company boundaries, locally each of the three principal SR constituent had slight differences in their operational requirements and which would affect attempts, particularly by Maunsell, to standardise locomotives and rolling stock across the system. The most notable of these were:

The LBSCR used Westinghouse air brakes whilst the other two used Vacuum brakes. This meant that locomotives had to work with the appropriately-equipped carriage stock, although the Southern rapidly standardised on the vacuum brake except on the Isle of Wight where the air brakes remained to the end of steam in 1966. LBSCR locomotives (and the LSWR O2s sent to the Island) had the Westinghouse pumps in prominent positions on the locomotives. Until the Southern conversions were completed a number of mainland engines, such as a pair of T9s, had Westinghouse pumps so they could operate with LBSCR stock.

The SECR had lines with severe loading gauge restrictions which resulted in special stock, the most restricted being the Tonbridge to Hastings line which gave rise both to flat-sided carriages of Maunsell 'Restriction 0' profile and to the banning of the use of many locomotive types over the line. The North Kent lines and LBSCR lines to Eastbourne and through Lewes tunnel were also restricted but these were eased by the Southern by 1939.

All these things gave the Southern its unique character. Its choice of green liveries for its locomotives, stock and infrastructure harmonised with its non-industrial nature and set it further apart from its contemporaries. Its pursuit of electrification also set it apart from those companies as it was by far and away the leading advocate of 'the juice' as a form of power for its trains, a corollary of which was that steam locomotive development became somewhat stilted until the Bulleid era. However, that shouldn't be taken as a criticism of Maunsell (the Southern's first CME) and his team. They were severely constrained by their limited budget and the necessity to make the best of what they had. The locomotives which were produced certainly had a great deal of charisma, as did the types inherited from the constituents, whose longevity was to further add to the character and legend of the Southern right up to the end of steam on British Railways. Many Southern engines in turn received the somewhat-dubious title of "the oldest working locomotive on British Railways", as did much of the locomotive-hauled passenger stock: but that just adds to the Southern's charm for modellers!

3 Southern Locomotives

I guess for most of us it's the locomotives which were the first things we noticed about the Southern. I know in my own case it was the first Rebuilt Merchant Navy, 35018 'British India Line', which passed the end of the garden during a party in February 1956 celebrating a friend's 9th birthday. A little while later I saw this strange looking beast on the cover of 'Trains Illustrated' on the W H Smiths stand on New Milton station and that became the first railway magazine I ever had (Mum bought it for me!).

Because locomotive are so important to modellers I'm going to go into some depth about their origins, appearance and working lives. If I did that for every type of locomotive that worked on the Southern it would exceed all the space available, so in this chapter I will describe those built by the Southern itself. However, I shall concentrate on Ready-to-Run models (including those most likely to appear as RTR models in the future) in this volume as those are the ones most modellers are most likely to acquire. (I know kit- and scratch-builders will say all are equally possible for modelling, but, quite frankly, if you are a scratch builder you will already know more about all things Southern than I ever will! But we will revisit the subject in a future volume and go into greater detail about locomotives unlikely to be available RTR). Chapter 8 describes those inherited by the company, again detailing r-t-r models. This is a story that will run and run!

Most modellers ask, at some time, "can I legitimately run x on my layout with y?" so the these chapters will attempt to show what each class was, on what duties it would generally work and where it would work them. It's not a blow-by-blow description of the locomotives but an indication of those matters which may be important when deciding which types to use with one another and what they should look like.

Unique to the Southern were the Bulleid pacific designs. This time No. 34064 is nearest the camera and we think that's No. 34041 behind. The long, thin shape of the Giesl Ejector is apparent in this view. This was the final development of the Bulleid concept as it improved the locomotive considerably. Intended to reduce spark-throwing it also resulted in a very useful increase in power. Preserved classmate 34092 'City of Wells' has one today.   Mark Abbott

The problem with any layout (or book) is the choice - do you include the everyday or the unusual? For this section we have decided to choose the latter, the intention being to give the modeller even more choice on what to run. So, do you think an LMS 8F might only be seen on the S & D or perhaps a cross London freight? Well think again, No. 48408 had just worked a Waterloo - Basingstoke semi-fact when recorded at its destination station. (The engine had been sent by the LMR to Eastleigh for repair, the SR subsequently deciding to purloin it for a while, ostensibly 'running in' but in reality covering a particular duty. We should not admit it too loudly, but apparently it performed rather well.) 48536 reached Bournemouth in 1957.And these was not the only strange visitors to be seen.....
(During WW2 a batch of the 8F class was built at Eastleigh for the LMS and may well have operated running-in turns around the area.)
Mark Abbott

Never say 'Never'. Clearly this is Bournemouth Central shed, the elevated signalbox giving the game away. The 2-6-2T from that 'other railway' had arrived from Weymouth simply because it needed turning and the turntable at the latter was briefly out of use. Even members of the 'Castle' class were regularly seen at both Weymouth and Salisbury whilst one reached Portsmouth (and was impounded at Fratton) and others were recorded being serviced at Eastleigh. There were at least two recorded visits to Bournemouth itself, although the most common GWR locomotives here were 'Halls' and 'Granges'. All of these (and the 8Fs) are available RTR   Mark Abbott

Southern Railway Locomotives: General Background

Southern locomotives were unlike those of the other railways. As mentioned above, there were plenty of really elderly steam ones, the result of the Company's electrification programme which left little capital to invest in more modern machines. Curiously, since the electrification was of suburban lines (at least in the early years), the only real need for steam engines was to handle long distance traffic, so the Southern's two Chief Mechanical Engineers, Richard Maunsell and Oliver Bulleid, mostly designed or adapted designs for larger steam locomotives. It's a curious fact that no small tank engines for passenger work, just 21 large ones (the 'Rivers', which didn't last long) and 23 goods tanks (the Ws and Zs) were produced during the whole of the Southern Railway's existence (we'll come back to Bulleid's attempt to produce a replacement for the pre-grouping engines!). Whilst the Great Western built no fewer than 863 of its standard class 57xx Pannier tanks from 1929 to 1948 the Southern Railway, throughout its existence, built (or bought) just 516 locomotives *in total!* This all led to a small fleet of immense variety and great longevity - exactly what the modeller wants as the basis of his fleet.

Steam locomotives are generally divided into types such as express passenger, mixed traffic, goods (or mineral) and shunting engines with sub-divisions within those categories such as local passenger, dock shunters, pull-push (the Southern's term, not mine) etc. On the Southern the divisions were far more blurred than on other railways, most engine types really being mixed traffic as the apparent 'express' locomotives would often be found on goods work (we'll come back to that in the chapter on goods traffic) and vice-versa.

A quick note or two here about numbers: normally herein references to locomotive numbers have (3x) shown in front of their first Southern number if they remained in use in the same general form into BR days. If just the Southern number is shown it indicates they only ran in that form in Southern Railway days. Southern numbers were originally the same as those inherited from the constituents, but with an 'A' prefix for ex SECR engines, a 'B' for LBSCR ones and an 'E' for LSWR and absorbed ones. From 1931 these letters were replaced by a 1 for SECR engines, a 2 for LBSCR and the 'E' was just removed for LSWR ones. The letters actually referred to the Works to which the class was allocated for repairs, A = Ashford, B = Brighton and E = Eastleigh. There were certain 'duplicate' numbers inherited from the LSWR which started with an '0' which was replaced by a 3. The Southern generally filled unused LSWR series numbers for its engines, although some ex-SECR lineage machines appeared with SECR-series numbers. Is that clear?! It was one of the most confusing numbering systems of any of the 'Big Four' railways, which was only made even more obscure by BR which renumbered the ex-'duplicate' engines to fill holes in the old LSWR series. To illustrate: Beattie 'Well Tank' no. 298 was built in 1874, 'duplicated' to 0298 in 1898, had a prefix from 1923 to become E0298, was renumbered to 3298 in 1935 and finally became BR 30587 in 1948, the number it bears today (some of the Adams 0-6-0s had even *more* complicated renumbering histories!). The dear old Isle of Wight was an oasis of calm amongst all of this, its engines having their own series with a 'W' prefix, which didn't refer to the Works like the other number series (they would have been 'R' numbers as they were repaired at Ryde Works), didn't lose the 'W' after 1931 and then still kept the 'W' into BR days! Of course, the engines transferred from the mainland got renumbered into the 'W' series on transfer, and back to their original mainland numbers when repatriated.

Southern liveries, especially in the early days of nationalisation, can be a minefield. Here's one of the Isle of Wight E1s, complete with name and IoW number, at Ventnor Town in 1949 with its 'Southern' ownership simply overpainted in what appears to be undercoat grey. The Island engines would keep their numbers, without the addition of 30,000, and their 'W' prefixes (which only appeared on the cast numberplates on the bunkers) throughout the Southern Railway and BR Southern Region periods. These goods tanks would be humbled by BR by loosing their passenger livery and receiving a simple plain black: the O2s received the full lined-black passenger livery.

The Maunsell 'Ns' ran all over the Southern system. Here, deep in Brighton territory at South Croydon on 11 July 1962, is one of the Government-built (but Southern erected) 'Woolworths', no. 31862, an engine modelled by Bachmann as the first of what might be called 'modern' 4mm scale models, heading a breakdown crane in the consist of a normal freight train. Breakdown cranes didn't just work in dedicated trains to scenes of accidents, they would be moved around the system for use during engineering possessions and for lifting heavy items such as bridges. They would also have to be taken to Works occasionally for overhaul, although most were allocated to adjacent locomotive depots and thus be on hand.
RCTS CH01849

Before looking at constituent companies' locomotives what follows are some details of those that the Southern Railway built itself, followed by the BR classes, the emphasis being on when they were introduced, where they worked and on what duties they were used, especially for those available from the main manufacturers. In summary, 516 locomotives were added to stock by the Southern Railway and their classes were: (those in bold are available RTR)

Maunsell class	N/N1	86
	H15	15
	N15	54
	L1	15
	LN	16
	S15	25
	U/U1	71 (21 of these were rebuilt from class K/K1 2-6-4 tanks)
	Z	8
	W	15
	V	40

	Diesel Shunter	3
	Q	20
Bulleid class	MN	20
	Electric	3
	Q1	40
	WC/BB	70 (40 more built by BR)
Bought in	L&B	1
	USA	14

Maunsell Classes N and N1 (available in 4mm scale from Bachmann)

These were the first true Maunsell locomotives, the first, no. (31)810, being produced for the SECR in 1917, so I'm including them all together here. The SECR built another 14, nos. (31)811-821/3-5, from 1920 to 1923, the last 3 being built by the Southern.

The slow construction was a result of the company's poverty and backlog of repair work following the Great War. These were 2-cylinder 2-6-0s designated class N, except for no. (31)822, which was modified during construction with 3 cylinders to become class N1. These engines were, naturally, allocated to Eastern Section sheds.

With 5' 6" drivers these were classified as 'mixed traffic' engines (see S15 below, which were 'goods engines' but had *bigger* wheels!) and were originally painted in 'battleship grey' livery on the SECR. The SR painted them in passenger green and BR gave them mixed traffic lined black (these liveries applied to *all* the N/N1 engines). The design had distinct echoes of both Midland Railway and GWR practice, as Maunsell had employed James Clayton from the former and Harry Holcroft from Swindon. The latter was responsible for the boiler design and the use of a 2-6-0 chassis, following experience with the Churchward Moguls of class 43xx, curiously the only Churchward design that wasn't part of his GWR standardisation scheme, just an amalgam of standard parts. However,

the N was designed as the basis of an SECR standardisation scheme and led to the class K tanks, the resultant U class moguls and the W class tanks; there was also a tentative proposal for a 2-8-0 tank variant. All shared the boiler design, which was restricted in its dimensions in order to keep the weight of the K class tanks within the Civil Engineer's limits. The result was a locomotive which could run over many secondary routes which were banned to the S15s and Urie-derived classes. The N1 three cylinder prototype was a result of Holcroft's experiments with derived valve gear.

The design was adopted by the Ministry of Supply after the First World War as a putative Standard design for what was expected to be a nationalised railway system. In the event, the railways were 'grouped' into four large private companies and no-one wanted the 100 locomotives the Ministry had caused to be built, but not assembled, at Woolwich Arsenal.

But, of course, they were standard with the ex-SECR locomotives acquired by the Southern in 1923 and

This time it is the portrayal of a Southern-built 'N' class 2-6-0, No. 31405. The Southern modeller really cannot have too many Maunsell 2-6-0s and 4-6-0s on the layout, although in the case of the smaller engines be warned, different batches were left or right hand drive so ensure the cab crew is positioned correctly! This one has the larger 4,000 gallon tender. Other points to note are the AWS battery box, metal plate behind the front coupling protecting the AWS receiver, electrification warning sign (on the smoke deflector) and headcode disc. All too often the latter is omitted. Finally, good BR workaday grime - engines of the type based at Exmouth Junction and used on Meldon ballast trains were often covered in a brownish dust.

were an ideal way to acquire a large number of new engines for a system which desperately needed them. The Southern bought 50 'kits' in 1924 at a knock-down price and numbered them A826-75 (later (31)826-75), assembling them at Ashford. Because they were cheap bargains from Woolwich it was natural that they soon became known as 'Woolworths'! Curiously, for the modeller, these N class locomotives were assembled from kits but the 00 gauge model can be bought ready-to-run! Perhaps it was appropriate that Bachmann chose this prototype for the first fine-scale ready-to-run 4mm scale model as the class was accepted as the Southern's standard mixed traffic type and was put to use right across the new system, all but 3 of these machines being allocated to the Western Section. In BR days they became the staple motive power on the 'Withered Arm' lines although they weren't seen very often on, or allocated to, the Bournemouth lines, which had the H15s for these duties (31814, for example, did appear at Bournemouth on 3 separate occasions - 4/9/54, 5/2/56 and 8/7/56).

One Ashford engine, no. A816, was subjected to an experiment which gave it a bizarre look from 1931 to 1935. This involved the fitting of a condenser and a square chimney! No. 1850 had Marshall valve gear in lieu of its Walchaerts gear from October 1933 to April 1934: it wasn't a success.

Unlike the Urie-derived classes, their tenders were unchanged throughout their lives, which saw them in service right up to the middle 1960s, the last going in June 1966. Their tenders were the 3,500 gallon flat-sided 6 wheeled tenders which became known as the Ashford 3,500 tenders, and this design was later used on the 4-6-0s as detailed above. The ex-SECR locos and the Woolworths were visually almost identical.

A final batch of 15 Ns, (3)1400-14, was built in 1932, with some alterations, to bring the class total to 80, numerically the largest Maunsell class. Curiously, in that year the Southern bought the last 17 'kits' from Woolwich but didn't use them to construct this batch, which were new-builds at Ashford. To give them a greater range on Western Section work they were fitted with 4,000 gallon Ashford tenders with turned-in tops acquired second-hand from the various 4-6-0s, the first seven engines being right hand drive as were the earlier machines, the last 8 being built with left hand drive, the Southern standard. However, all the tenders had right hand fireman's fittings until Bulleid produced a batch of 8 new left hand tenders.

By 1933 the class was spread across the Southern, being shedded at Battersea (8 - all Woolworths), Bricklayers Arms (19 - 2 '14s' 11 SECR 6 W), Ashford (7 - 6 '14s' 1 SECR), New Cross Gate (2 - SECR),

Reading (1 - W), Redhill (2 - 1 '14' 1 SECR), Exmouth Jct (33 - 4 '14s', 1 SECR 28 W), Barnstaple (4 - W) and Salisbury (4 - 2 '14s' 2 W). The only notable change in their appearance during their long lives was the fitting of smoke deflectors from 1934 (nos. 1407-14 had them from new), the removal of the smoke box 'snifting valves' (this was common to all Maunsell classes) and the use of U1 class chimneys on some locomotives from 1937 onwards and finally BR Standard class 4 chimneys from 1957. From 1955 onwards a number of engines received new cylinders with outside steam pipes: the first of these, no 31848, ran for from October 1955 to the end of 1956 *without* smoke deflectors. By 1958 the allocations were Bricklayers Arms 16, Ashford 10, Hither Green 7, Gillingham 2, Faversham 1, Dover 4, Stewarts Lane 10, Redhill 9, Salisbury 2 and Exmouth Jct 19.

The Ns were long-lived: the first, no. 31409, was withdrawn in November 1962 (and was the shortest-lived of the class!) and the last, its immediate 'sister', 31408, in June 1966.

Bachmann have produced almost every variant of this large class, the only exception being the final 8 engines with left hand drive. They refer to the 4,000 gallon tenders as 'slope-sided' tenders.

The solitary modified N1, (31)822, showed little improvement over the standard Ns but its cylinder layout allowed it to work over the Tonbridge to Hastings line over which the Ns were barred. Therefore, in 1930, the Southern built a further 5 N1s, nos. (3)1876-80 although no more N1s were produced subsequently as the U1 locomotives proved to be more versatile, a reverse of the experience elsewhere on Southern metals. The prototype had a 3,500 gallon tender and the production batch had 4,000 gallon flat-sided ones.

In general, their appearance and details followed the Ns, although they remained on Eastern and Central Section duties throughout their service days, no. 822 working from Ashford in 1924 and Bricklayers Arms thereafter until it joined the other 5 at New Cross when they were built. In the 1930s they were variously stationed at Tonbridge, Eastbourne and the London sheds.

All became BR engines and were then split between St Leonards (2) and Hither Green (4). The latter used one regularly on a morning passenger working but heavy goods, notably on the Hastings line, remained their forte, combined with weekend excursion work to the Kent coast resorts.

Withdrawals followed Kent Coast electrification, the entire class going by November 1962.

Maunsell 'King Arthur' class N15 4-6-0 (available in 4mm scale from Hornby)

These were a development of Urie's class N15 of which there were 20 built for the LSWR (see later below). The Southern ones split into 3 varieties, all of which Hornby have modelled.

The first was a batch of 10, numbers (30)448 to (30) 457, known as the 'Eastleigh Arthurs', as they were built at the old LSWR Works there in 1925. They were replacements for unsuccessful Drummond G14 and P14 4-6-0s although they used few parts from them except their tenders, which were the well-known 'Watercart' 8-wheeled bogie tenders with inside axle boxes, modified to hold 4,300 gallons of water. The first built was (30)453 which was named 'King Arthur', giving its name to the whole class, although the LSWR designation of N15 was the official name. (Maunsell didn't like his engines, which had major alterations of

the steam passages and valve gear, being associated with the Urie N15s, although they were physically almost identical). These engines had cabs identical to the Urie ones and could not work on either the Central or Eastern Divisions. The 'Watercart' tenders were gradually replaced with standard 5,000 gallon 8-wheel bogie Urie tenders ('Urie tenders' from hereon) during the 1950s as older Urie engines were withdrawn. Hornby have produced both tender variants in BR livery. These 10 engines spent almost their entire careers at Salisbury depot, working on the West of England main line.

The next batch was a series of 40 locomotives built by the North British Locomotive Co. of Glasgow in 1925 which incorporated the Maunsell modifications together with an improved cab (the 'Ashford' cab) which fitted the combined Southern loading gauge, although they were banned from the Tonbridge to Hastings line. As delivered, they were rather less

'Maunsell 'King Arthurs' could still be seen on Pullmans in BR days! The 'Kentish Belle' (formerly known as the 'Thanet Belle' from its introduction under BR in 1948) ran to Ramsgate via Chatham and consisted of just 8 Pullmans. In it first year as the 'Kentish Belle' in 1951 it detached 3 cars at Faversham for Canterbury although it was for that season alone. However, the other 5 cars would make a classic short rake for a modeller as most Pullman services tended to be 10 to 12 cars long.*
Here we see 30763 'Sir Bors de Ganis', in early emblem BR express passenger green at the head of the train which ceased to run when the first phase of the Kent Coast electrification came into play in 1959, its last years being normally the province of Bulleid Light Pacifics.
                                                                                          RCHS/Spence Collection

satisfactory than the 'Eastleigh Arthurs', which was traced to shoddy workmanship rather than design. These engines, (30)763 to (30)792, were known as the 'Scotch Arthurs' or 'Scotchmen' (for obvious reasons), fitted with Urie tenders and were deployed on both the Western and Eastern Divisions, changing little in their lifetimes other than occasional tender swaps and the fitting of smoke deflectors from the 1930s onwards (as were all the Maunsell 4-6-0s, 4-4-0s and 2-6-0s - this won't be repeated in every description). 763-8/70-2 were fitted with 6 wheel 4,000 gallon tenders of Ashford design from 1928 to 1930-odd and flat-sided 8 wheel tenders thereafter until 1931/2 but then ran the rest of their careers with the Urie pattern ones. They handled all the principal express trains on the Eastern Section main lines to Dover and Ramsgate and the Bournemouth and West of England trains on the Western Section, dominating the line beyond Salisbury together with the Eastleigh Arthurs.

The final batch of 14 engines, (30)793 to (30)806, didn't have a nickname, but had small 6-wheel tenders of Ashford design carrying just 3,500 gallons. These were fitted to allow the engines to work on the Central Division which had short turntables. They also necessitated a change in the drawgear as a result of which when fitted with redundant Urie tenders in the late 1950s the tender and locomotive footplate heights didn't match. These engines had charge of the principal Brighton expresses until 1933 and the Continental boat trains to Newhaven for some time

thereafter. One, no. 30796, still with its little tender, was seen on an up goods train at Boscombe in July 1953.

All the N15s were used on expresses in Southern Railway days, and even under BR(SR) were to be seen on main line trains. They didn't appear on secondary lines or branches as they were built 'like battleships', a legacy of Urie's design principles. They were banned beyond Exeter so didn't appear on the 'Withered Arm' lines and none was allocated west of Salisbury in BR days. Some of the Central Section ones were re-allocated to the Eastern Section after the Brighton main line was electrified in 1933 and then to the Western Section in 1959 upon the Kent Coast electrification, when 8 of them received Urie tenders. They did, however, regularly stray from Southern metals, principally to Oxford on Inter-Regional workings over ex-GWR metals. They also headed many a Pullman train, notably the 'Southern Belle' to Brighton, the 'Bournemouth Belle' in its early days and the 'Kentish Belle' in BR days.

The full history of these locomotives is fascinating and complicated: the above is a general outline to give the modeller a basic understanding of which ones may be appropriate to his layout. Perhaps the most significant point is how few lines saw them. The complete history makes a very detailed book and there is a number of such books available to give the exact data. Of course, this applies to all the locomotive types which follow!

Maunsell Class S15 4-6-0

These were the freight version of the N15s, again an improved Urie design. The Southern built 15, (30)823-37, in 1927/8 and 10 more, (30)838-47, in 1936, these being the only main line goods locomotives built by the railway. As pointed out earlier, they were really mixed traffic engines and would be found on most types of passenger trains except the expresses as well as on the heaviest goods trains. (As an aside, the Southern never had any 8-coupled tender engines of its own, although both its CMEs as well as Drummond and Urie of the LSWR drew up plans for such engines at one time or another, Bulleid intending his for passenger work after his experiences with Gresley's famous 'Cock O' The North' class P2 2-8-2s).

The Maunsell S15s had the later 'Ashford' cabs and were all the same except for their tenders, changes to which were complicated. The first 10 had Urie tenders (the second 5 sporting vacuum cylinders on the back for their first year only) whilst the other 15 had flush-sided versions of these. However, 5 flush-sided ones from 833-7 were soon (in1928) transferred to 'Lord Nelsons' and, after 7 years with Urie tenders, these engines received Ashford 4,000 gallon 6 wheel tenders in 1936 for use on the Central Division. 838-42 went to Hither Green when new, the only ones to be allocated to the Eastern Section. They were transferred to the Western Section at the end of 1942 after which they all remained on the old LSWR lines until after Nationalisation.

In 1950 30835-7 went to Redhill and were used on trains to Ashford, the only time these engines were allocated to Eastern Division services. In 1960 they were joined by 30847, which became the only member of the class to work with an Ashford 3,500 gallon tender. The only other tender variation was the fitting of 'Schools' 4,000 gallon tenders to 30833/7 in 1962, these having turned-in raves at the top, the earlier 6-wheel tenders all being flat-sided. 30837 was probably the most-photographed member of the class as it was used on a pair of 'S15 Commemorative' rail tours in early 1966, the last Maunsell 4-6-0 locomotive to work for BR.

The true nature of these 'goods' engines can be divined from the fact that the first 15 bore the goods black livery when built but the last 10 appeared in full passenger livery, and the earlier ones were then also painted green. BR weren't quite so kind to them and painted them plain black, but that didn't stop the Southern Region from using them on passenger trains, including some of the Ocean Liner 'expresses' on summer Saturdays.

It seems highly likely that a ready-to-run model will be produced, and it should be noted that they are not simply an N15 with smaller drivers! (they are shorter, so don't try and modify an N15 to produce an S15: be patient!).

Opposite - *A theme which will become apparent during this book is the use of 'express' locomotives on non-passenger work. This is another 'Scotch Arthur' seen at Brockenhurst on 17 June 1959 with a train of empty Meldon Hoppers on their way back home.* *RCTS CH00217*

Here's a 'proper' Southern goods engine, an S15. This is the first of Maunsell's final batch of 10 built in 1936, adorned in Bulleid's austerity livery, having been outshopped in Maunsell passenger livery as noted above. Note the vacuum tanks just showing on the rear of the tender. This was the only batch to have gone when new to the Eastern Division. RCHS/Spence Collection

No. (30)864 'Sir Martin Frobisher' posed for an official portrait - what a pity the backgrounds were invariably wiped out. Light green livery, but wartime modifications with the cab side window blanked out and runners for blackout screens between the engine and tender. When clean this livery was superb, although the debate continues on the merits of the green smoke defectors.

Maunsell Class LN 'Lord Nelson' 4-6-0 (available in 4mm scale from Bachmann)

This design was Maunsell's 'magnum opus', but has a rather tarnished reputation. The prototype, no. (30)850 'Lord Nelson', was built in 1926 and was briefly the most powerful passenger locomotive in Great Britain, based on tractive effort. However, the effort of getting the power onto the road was too much. But the LMS must have been impressed as they requested copies of the working drawings so they could ask the North British Locomotive Company to build them a 3-cylinder version of this 4-cylinder design, which became the 'Royal Scots'. How much of the 'Nelson' design actually was incorporated in the 'Scot' is open to debate!

The design was drawn up to meet a specification for a locomotive powerful enough to pull Eastern Section Continental Expresses weighing 500 tons at an average speed of 55 mph, without resort to double-heading, an aim not fully realised. It was also intended to cover the Western Section expresses to the West Country and Bournemouth, on which modest success was achieved. The prototype remained a singleton for two years until 15 production versions were built in

1928-29. The design incorporated an unusual 8 exhaust beats per revolution, as most 4-cylinder locomotives gave 4 beats. The 8 beats gave a soft exhaust and made the engines sound as though they were going at twice the normal speed. Of course, historically this has been irrelevant to modellers but the advent of DCC sound systems makes it an important fact for future modelling!

The early history and the variations in the class are extremely complicated. Suffice it to say that the only external differences were the fitting of a single extra-long boiler to (30)860 (in BR days it also was used on 30852/5), a massive round-top boiler to (30)857 in 1937 (it was experimental as the design was being considered for proposed Pacific and 4-8-0 goods locomotive types, both based on the LN design) and 6' 3" driving wheels on (30)859 instead of the standard 6' 7" ones on the rest of the class. For his 4-6-0s Maunsell had followed the Urie (and his predecessors' on the LSWR) tradition regarding wheel sizes. One other little quirk about this class was its official designation, class LN, which was out of step with the single letter classification which Maunsell had otherwise followed directly on from his SECR days.

Opposite - *The Bulleid changes to the 'LNs' are seen on 'Lord Nelson' himself, rounding the curve from Gasworks Junction to Bournemouth West from Central with a train consisting of the first of Bulleid's six-car sets for the Bournemouth line, no 290. The extended sides of the Maunsell tender, fitted to make them 'self-trimming' and the wide chimney to take the exhaust from the multiple blastpipe are both prominent as are the vacuum cylinders on the rear platform, which were fitted during Maunsell's tenure. Although best known in BR days for their time at Eastleigh, a number of LNs spent the early part of the nationalisation era based at Bournemouth and had regular turns to the town until the very end. The division of trains at Central into portions for Weymouth and the west termi-nus meant that this was another location where 'model-length' trains might be seen behind almost any type of lo-comotive, from M7 tanks to Merchant Navies.*

The types of tender used in the early days were slightly complicated and it was the 'Nelsons' which precipitated the cascade of tenders amongst the 4-6-0 classes. It was realised that the long engine-and-tender length of the class made it difficult to use on the Eastern Section with its short turntables. All were built with the handsome flat-sided 8 wheel tender but nos. 852/3 went to work with Ashford 4,000 gallon 6 wheel tenders and then, after less than 18 months, received the standard Urie style ones with flared tops, as did 858/9/60 from new. All 5 then got the standard flat sided 8 wheeler in 1931-2 and this remained the standard for the rest of their existence.

The engines were divided between the Eastern and Western Sections throughout the 1930s, with rather more on the latter, although the numbers varied year by year. When first built they penetrated as far as Exeter but tended to run short of steam on the long climbs. As a result they were kept east of Salisbury, becoming the standard top link power for the Bournemouth road until outclassed by the 'Schools'. The steaming problem was attributed to poor exhaust arrangements and the long firegrate, which was partly sloping and partly level, which echoed the shape of those in the Drummond 4-6-0s which no-one ever seemed to like. Even the Salisbury men couldn't get to grips with them, although they had some experience of this type of grate with the H15 rebuilds. Other railways

used this arrangement extensively and it's thought that the relative scarcity of the 16 'Nelsons' accounted for this problem - no crews had sufficient time to get acquainted with their foibles.

Maunsell kept trying to cure them but his retirement in 1937 handed the baton over to the mercurial Oliver Bulleid who set about the 'Nelsons' with gusto. First he fitted upper side-sheets to the tenders to make them self-trimming. Then he used them to experiment with multiple blast pipes and wide chimneys. These alterations transformed the engines both in appearance and performance, tests showing them to be far more free-running than before.
Then the War came and all locomotives just had to earn their keep. Under the cover of the War Bulleid introduced his 'mixed traffic' locomotives and when it ended the Southern found it had dozens of flat-sided things which could work, at least in theory, all the fast trains, so the 'Nelsons' were somewhat sidelined. One thing the 'Nelsons' always exhibited was great reliability, a total contrast to the Bulleid engines. By this time they were all on the Western Section, divided between Nine Elms, Eastleigh and Bournemouth and when the new national railway concern was trying to find a standard livery for its engines the 'Nelsons', which had sported all the Southern's panoply of passenger liveries, were chosen to try out an apple green version on 30856/61/4. They kept it for a couple

of years and then became Brunswick green as they were classified 7P under BR's power classification scheme.

Through the 1950s things remained the same except that Nine Elms gave its members of the class up to Eastleigh where, completing the circle of their design specification, they found a final role as locomotives for the various Ocean Liner Expresses from Southampton Docks, as well as making visits to the Western Region at Oxford. All were withdrawn in the holocaust year of 1962 when the Southern disposed of many classes of perfectly good locomotives at the stroke of the accountant's pen.

The 'Nelsons' final fling was on the Ocean Liner Expresses from Southampton Docks, for which they bore some spectacular headboards. Many of these were found in a shed at Eastleigh at the end of steam and are today cherished treasures.

<u>Maunsell Class V 'Schools' express passenger 4-4-0</u> (available in 4mm scale from Hornby)

If the 'Nelsons' were a disappointment, their progeny were the exact opposite. Faced with a requirement for a powerful but cheaper-to-build express passenger engine in the straightened circumstances of the early 1930s Maunsell combined the best features of the 'Nelsons' and 'King Arthurs' to produce what was to be the most powerful 4-4-0 in Europe. The chassis was effectively a 'Nelson' one with a pair of drivers removed along with one cylinder. On top of it was a

Seen at Ramsgate in the 1930s 'Whitgift' bore a chimney without the prominent capuchon usual on Maunsell's elegant chimneys. The lack of this feature makes a tremendous difference to the 'look' of the engine. It goes to show that the modeller should always take the oft-repeated advice 'Get a photo of the prototype at the time you wish to model it'.

shortened 'King Arthur' round-top boiler and firebox with a normal sloping grate, the resulting engine being of a slim enough profile to be acceptable on even the Tonbridge to Hastings line. The product of this

This is probably one of the services for which the 'Schools' are best remembered: an Eastern Section express on the Chatham route at Wandsworth Road. It consists of a mixture of SECR 'Continental' stock and Maunsell's narrow-bodied 'Restriction 0' or 'Restriction 1' coaches for Eastern Section services, both the Chatham and Hastings lines originally having width issues. In the middle is a Pullman Car: a number of narrow-bodied Pullmans were built for the Hastings line.

marriage was one of the most outstanding locomotives of all time. Contrary to popular myth, they weren't designed for the Hastings line and were even banned from it at first due to platform clearances and by being overweight for some of the bridges, which had to be strengthened.

Three batches were built, the first 10, (30)900-09, in 1930, which were set to work on the Central Section from Eastbourne and the Eastern Section from Dover. A further 30 appeared (slowly) between 1932 and 1935, the running numbers being (30)910 to (30)939. 10 more were ordered but cancelled. The Hastings line first saw them in mid-1931 and once the whole class had been delivered they were shedded at St Leonards, Ramsgate, Fratton and Eastbourne, working the principal services on the Hastings, North Kent, Portsmouth and Eastbourne lines. The latter soon lost them as it was electrified in July 1935 and Fratton bid farewell to them two years later for the same reason. The Eastbourne ones went to Bricklayers Arms and the Fratton ones to Bournemouth. Here they became famous for their use on the fastest service on the line, the 'Bournemouth Limited', a service which only saw them for two years as it was withdrawn when war broke out.

This was a busy time however, as Bulleid was tinkering with the class. He had 'Sevenoaks' dressed

up in a plywood streamlined cowling, although it only made one short run, from Eastleigh to Winchester, with it in place. He also started to fit his Lemaître multiple blast pipes and wide chimneys to the class but to no real effect so stopped after disfiguring half of the class. He also altered one of the tenders by giving it a self-trimming coal space and extended sides but it wasn't necessary on such a short tender and wasn't repeated. Otherwise all the engines shared the same design of Ashford 4,000 gallon tender with angled top sheeting albeit with minor differences such as disc wheels on some and a different layout of toolboxes on the final 30. The self-trimmer ran behind (30)932 'Blundell's' until 1958 when it was transferred to 30905. Two engines, 30912 and 30921, received 'Lord Nelson' tenders during 1961 (which suited them very well) and ran with them until withdrawal at the end of the following year. Both these engines were painted BR Brunswick green, a livery which was applied to all but four of the class after 1956, prior to which they had worn, in order, Maunsell's attractive olive green, Bulleid's coats of many colours and BR mixed traffic lined black, a most inappropriate colour for what were always express passenger locomotives *par excellence* (but even they were to be seen on goods traffic occasionally . . .)

Returning to their activities, at the end of the War they were gathered on the Eastern Section except for 3 at

27

I've included this tender view of no. 30923 'Bradfield' (and a number of other such views throughout the book) as most photos are of front three-quarters aspects of locomotives and modellers need to see all angles to be able to 'get it right'. This picture also shows the 'illegal' BR crest introduced in 1956 with the lion facing to the right. The custodians of British heraldry told BR they could only use the left-facing lion and thus from 1959 onwards the lion on the right side of locomotives looked backwards!

Bournemouth and one at Basingstoke. The Bournemouth ones went to Brighton in 1946 and by 1949 they were all on the Eastern Division. However, they still appeared elsewhere, such as 30912 at Bournemouth on 9/7/53. A few moved around a bit to sheds such as Eastbourne but the next big move came in 1957 when the Hastings Dieselisation started. 30903-7 went to Nine Elms and once again became common at Bournemouth. Thereafter the Kent Coast

electrification spelt the end for them although most eked out their twilight years on the Western Division with forays on the West of England main line and their well-known use on the Summer Saturday Lymington Pier through trains. Withdrawal started with 30919 in January 1961 and most were swept away in the mass withdrawal of November 1962 which saw their final demise.

Bulleid Class MN (Merchant Navy) 4-6-2 (available in 4mm scale from Hornby in Rebuilt form)

When Bulleid took over from Maunsell in 1937 no-one could have foreseen what in direction his design skills would take the Southern. Like his mentor at the LNER, Sir Nigel Gresley, he was a died-in-the-wool steam man and believed that the steam locomotive had a great deal more development ahead of it. There was

some logic to this as the A4s had only just been built at this time and coal was an indigenous fuel whilst oil had to be expensively imported for the new-fangled diesels.

At first he tinkered with Maunsell engines as detailed earlier but it wasn't until the War was well under way that he showed his hand, using the War restrictions to justify the outline of his first exhibit, the notorious - or

Left - *My first memory of any model locomotive is of a BR blue Graham Farish 'Merchant Navy' (together with a malachite green one) in the window of a model shop next to the Grand Cinema in Westbourne, a stone's throw both from my birthplace and Bournemouth West station. Although no RTR model of an original MN is currently available, I think this justifies the inclusion of this photo! Curiously, many of us have seen 'Canadian Pacific' in this paint scheme in recent times as the preserved (and rebuilt) engine has worn it. Hornby even released a model of the locomotive in this state, but, to clarify matters no 'Merchant Navy' ran in BR blue in its rebuilt form in service. Here the engine stands outside Eastleigh shed shortly before it entered the Works for a full General Overhaul in January 1954 when it would lose the blue paintwork for standard BR green. At its following General in 1959 it would be rebuilt.*

Above - *This is how I remember them in later days. 'East Asiatic Company' is seen being serviced at the small depot at Branksome, inside the triangle of lines between Gasworks Jct, Branksome station and Bournemouth West Jct. Most people associate the shed with the Somerset & Dorset, as its locomotives were shedded there overnight and S&D crews worked from it. However, it was a Southern shed and its most important duty was to service the Nine Elms 'Merchant' that brought the 'Bournemouth Belle' to the town at just before 3 pm and then took it back to London just after 4.30pm. It was the heaviest train on the line and was one of the few Bournemouth expresses without a Weymouth portion, the complete train running to and from the West station. Hornby's 'new era' started with models of the 'Merchant Navy' and Pullmans that made up the 'Bournemouth Belle'.*

glorious - 'Merchant Navy' class Pacific engines. Eyes accustomed to the elegance of British locomotive design could hardly be believed when they were set upon this slab-sided apparition, the first of which appeared in early 1941. It wore a bright malachite green livery with gunmetal nameplates and number plates bearing the indecipherable number 21C1. The path to this design was complicated, Bulleid having proposed a 2-8-2 in the first instance although the old fear of leading pony trucks at speed and the long coupled wheelbase had scotched the idea.

Of course we all got used to the appearance and many, me included, revere the 'Spamcan' look. 10, numbered 21C1-10, were built in the early War years and brought cries of indignation from observers who thought that they were out-and-out express passenger locomotives produced at a time of wartime austerity when 'what was wanted' was goods engines. But Bulleid declared that they were mixed traffic engines, a claim that has been laughed out of court down the years.

However, the evidence shows that Bulleid was right. The Southern was unlike the other railways, since passenger traffic was its principal revenue source. As a result passenger traffic was given priority during the day but was light at night. Therefore goods traffic was concentrated into the hours of darkness wherever possible, especially the long distance trains. Virtually all Southern steam locomotives were used at some time on goods traffic, as some of the photographs in this book illustrate. The big Pacifics did more than their fair share of this work, proving invaluable on the overnight fast freights from the West Country and then hauling troop trains and ambulance trains throughout the War years. I'll go into much more detail in the goods traffic chapter.

The first 10 MNs were joined by numbers 21C11-20 in 1945, all of which were available to assist in the D-Day landings and their aftermath. The locomotives showed many changes from the first batch, which were gradually altered to come into line. This phase of the class history is incredibly complicated, as each

We all know that Bulleid was derided for his claim that the 'Merchants' were mixed traffic engines, but they had regular freight duties throughout their working lives. Here we see 35010 'Blue Star' in her final form in the 1960s on a down West of England freight, passing another Southern mixed traffic machine, U class mogul 31798, one of the former 'Rivers', also once looked upon as a passenger type. The latter is standing in the London end sidings which still exist today at Yeovil Junction, and the Pacific is about to run into the down platform, no doubt to be overtaken by a classmate on the ACE or another WoE express on the down through line. Judging by the bauxite liveries of the wagons, this is a fully fitted express freight, so it justifies the use of a powerful and fast Pacific.   Bruce Oliver

From the bridge at the east end of Exeter Central 'Orient Line' is near the end of its journey from Waterloo. Its train will be split into North Devon, Plymouth and North Cornwall portions, unless this is a Summer Saturday, when the whole train might go through to North Devon. Usually the catering vehicles were detached/attached at Exeter Central, the carriage sidings to the right servicing these. Cyril Freezer once prepared a layout plan for Exeter Central, in his book 'Plans for Larger Layouts', the incredible amount of workings here would make a very interesting project! 'Merchants' were banned beyond here, the 'Light Pacifics' (that's 34086 '219 Squadron' in the background) working trains on over Great western metals at St David's station onto the 'Withered Arm'. Central saw a huge variety of locomotives, including Ws, Zs, E1Rs, M7s, G6s, O2s and BR Standard class 3 tanks as well as various Maunsell 2-6-0s and 4-6-0s and their BR replacements and equivalents. Carriage stock included the famous Bulleid 'Tavern Cars' the 'Devon Belle' Pullmans, the multi-portioned 'Atlantic Coast Express' with its many BCKs and even the 'Car-Carrier' which used the only SR green BE GUV vans. Cyril Freezer was right: it would make an amazing model - it's even got tunnels at each end. Who's going to do it? David Smith

locomotive would look different almost every time it was seen, a nightmare (or fascination) for modellers!

A third batch was commenced in the first year of nationalisation to give a class total of 30. These were delivered as 35021-30, as BR would have none of Bulleid's clumsy alpha-numeric system and the earlier ones became 35001-20.

It would take an entire book to detail all the changes of appearance to the locomotives (and there many of them already out there) so I shall bottle out here and refer the reader to any of the Merchant Navy monologues that are available today. Having said that, here are a few generalities: there were three tender

designs, each batch having different ones. The first batch had 5,000 gallon ones, the second 5,100 gallon ones and the final batch 6,000 gallon ones on a longer wheelbase. All had 'raves' - high, enclosed sides. In BR days the 'raves' were progressively cut-down starting with three engines in 1952, although most were done at the time of rebuilding the locomotives. One 6,000 gallon tender was converted by BR to weigh coal, also in 1952. It, and most of the others, was moved from one locomotive to another quite frequently: Eastleigh seemed to take an almost fiendish delight in playing 'musical tenders' - some of the engines even started life with the wrong tender!

The locomotives themselves changed appearance

quite significantly. The first batch had a 'widow's peak' at the top of the smoke box/ front of the casing and no smoke deflectors. Later, vestigial deflectors (of a number of shapes and sizes), then full deflectors and, on 21C20 massively-long deflectors, were fitted. Even once a standard style of deflector was decided upon some were flat and some gently curved. The 'widow's peak' gave way to a cowl and the positioning and number of safety valves varied from three to two and from in front of to behind the (hidden) dome. The cab shape and number of sliding window panes also varied.

cause of so much excitement to the young me. It appeared in January 1956 and was used for some while on the "Bournemouth Belle". The first 11 had the early BR 'cycling lion' on their tenders, whilst all the rest had the later crest, four with the 'incorrect' or 'illegal' right-facing one (not modelled by Hornby). They were variously shedded at Nine Elms, Bournemouth, Salisbury and Exmouth Junction in the 1950s and early 60s. As steam operation drew to a close many were shedded at Weymouth in those dark hours. In the early days of their new persona the tendency was for them to be used on Bournemouth

The inevitable rear three-quarter view, of 35012 'United States Lines' at Waterloo shows how the glow from the firebox shows up even on a bright day. Triang-Hornby used to offer locomotives with a 'firebox glow' feature which was regarded as a bit of a gimmick, but modern desires to recreate as much of the experience of the steam engine through DCC might see it make a comeback, as may smoke: there are 'real coal smoke' oils for smoke units these days which don't have that rather acrid and greasy texture that the early such units gave off. However, we still await brown smoke oil like that hanging around the front end of this Pacific. The 1960s towers in the background might be an inspiration for half-relief scenery. Lawrence Hassall

Their operational envelope was quite restricted, they only ever worked regularly on the main lines from Waterloo to Bournemouth and Exeter and on the Eastern Division on the Continental Boat Trains (for which they were originally specified à la the LNs). There were usually one or two on the latter duties, the last two to remain in their original condition working their final days there. No Rebuilt MNs worked on the Eastern Division.

Which brings us to the Rebuilds, which are probably of more interest to modellers due to the fact that there is a superb model available in 4mm scale, as referred to in the Introduction.

There has been much controversy over the term with which to describe the Pacifics in their two forms. As conceived by Bulleid they are variously referred to as 'Originals', 'Spamcans', 'Flat-tops' or 'Unrebuilts' (or by any number of unrepeatable names!), the BR versions being called 'Rebuilds' or 'Modified' engines. All are perfectly acceptable, bar the term 'Unrebuilt', which would imply that an engine has been rebuilt and then unrebuilt, something which has never happened to a 'Merchant', despite at least one preservation era scheme to 'unrebuild' 35022.

The first Rebuild was 35018 'British India Line', the

line trains with the Originals that remained being used to Exeter or on the Eastern Division. However, the 'ACE' was usually a Rebuild turn, which meant that they did regular freight workings from the start.

Once rebuilt, all were virtually identical except for their tenders, which continued to exhibit new features over time. There was one locomotive exception, good old 35018, which had different pipework along the boiler sides and to the clack valves and longer sand fillers: it was never brought into line with the rest of the class. The engines only had one livery, Brunswick green, although that could seldom be seen under the layers of grime on them at the end. And some of them remained to the very end, which came on 9th July 1967 when 35030, the last 'Merchant' built, brought the last steam-hauled passenger train service of the Southern into London.

Members of the class strayed occasionally from their well-trodden paths. In 1956 the pioneer 35018 ran from Nine Elms to Brighton for attention and worked back with ECS from Hassocks to Selhurst. In June 1957, when 3 months old as a Rebuild, 35017 worked a boat train from Newhaven Harbour to Victoria vice a failed Bulleid Electric loco, having been on hand as a result of tests conducted between Redhill and Three

Two views of the first Rebuilt Bulleid Pacific, 35018 'British India Line' shortly after being released to traffic when it was an inspiration to me. These pictures show the pipework on each side of the boiler which was unique to this engine. On the left hand side the two pipes along the boiler kinked downwards in front of the nameplate and on the right (below) the pipes supplying the boiler feed clacks were kinked above the running boards. On both sides the sandboxes had longer feedpipes and were kinked in a strange way. The photo below was taken on 31 March 1956 at Bournemouth West, the engine being the regular power for the 'Bournemouth Belle' until the second Rebuild, no. 35020, came along at the beginning of May. Note the 6-wheel bogie of the leading Pullman Car.
RCHS/Spence Collection and RCTSJAY1668

Another Bulleid double-header - a complete Bulleid train - on 11 June 1960 at Holes Bay Jct The leading engine is a 'West Country', 34028 'Eddystone', a survivor today. It is in pretty filthy condition for 1960, with its cabside number rather ostentatiously cleaned. Weathering isn't just for 'end of steam' models! The train engine is 35021 'New Zealand Line' and they are on the 1550 Weymouth to Waterloo service, the stock of which is another of the Bournemouth 6-car sets. Another eminently reproducible train!   *RCTS CH00550*

Bridges. Railtours took them places too: the earliest was 35022 which worked an Ian Allan Trains Illustrated special over the Western's Devon main line, climbing Hemerdon and Rattery banks with aplomb in 1958 on its way from Plymouth to Paddington (not that that is relevant to the Southern - there were other tours to other Regions, but I'm not going to cover them). On Southern metals 35007 ran from Littlehampton to Brighton and then up the main line to Victoria in 1964 whilst 35011 ran up the S&D from Broadstone to Templecombe on what should have been its penultimate day of existence on 1st January 1966. Curiously, 35028 did a trip from Victoria to Redhill, Guildford, Staines and Clapham Jct on 5th June 1966 - almost exactly the route it takes many times a year today on the 'Surrey Luncheon Expresses' for VSOE!

The Rebuilt Merchant Navy class is as iconic a Southern institution as any, but although they only had 11 years work on the SR in service days, how many Southern enthusiasts can resist them? There are probably more 'Bournemouth Belle' models running on layouts than any other well-known named train!

<u>Bulleid Classes WC and BB (West Country and Battle of Britain) 4-6-2</u> (available in 4mm scale from Hornby in both Original and Rebuilt forms)

The final Bulleid design built by the Southern was the most numerous and, in typical Bulleid fashion, had the most complicated official class designation. Although all 110 locomotives were essentially the same, they were split into two classes purely on the basis of their names - two locomotives actually changed class simply by having their names changed! A simpler designation which many enthusiasts use is 'Light Pacifics' as they were designed to be a slightly less weighty version of the Merchant Navy design, capable of working on most parts of the system, even many branch lines.

To ensure authenticity, modellers need to be aware of the many apparently-minor alterations these engines were subject to throughout their lives, most of which are present in Hornby's splendid models.

The first, 21C101 'Exeter', appeared in the dying days of the War and looked almost identical to the MNs.

From June 1945 to November 1947 Brighton Works was kept busy as a continuous stream of no less than 70 nearly-identical Pacifics were churned out. Identical except for the names. The first 50 were to be named after towns, cities and geographical features of the West Country which the Southern system served and the next 20 after personalities, aircraft and squadrons involved in the Battle of Britain. Much refining of the names meant that two more locomotives were needed to satisfy protocol for the latter series of names so the first 48 were WCs and the last 22 BBs. Numbers 21C149/50 were WCs while they being built but emerged as BBs! (Irrelevant, I know, but fascinating - 21C149 was to have been 'Saunton Sands' and 21C150 'Lorna Doone').

There were only two major changes to their appearance during the production of these engines: the size of the smoke deflectors and the layout of the cab windows: in time they would all get the modifications. The only way to tell which class a locomotive belonged to was by its number or the shape of the nameplate and shield or crest. The numbers followed the Bulleid pattern up to no. 21C170, these being changed to 34001 to 34070 by BR. A brief change to nos. 21C119 and 34036 was the fitting of oil firing for a few months in 1947/8 which was mostly notable for the oil tanks in the coal space of the tenders.

A 'BB' in original condition. 34073 is one of the final 40, with wider cabs and 5,500 gallon tenders and was appropriately working on the Eastern Division. Some people regard them as the 'true' 'Battle of Britain' class, but the reality is that all 110 engines were of one type and are best described simply as 'Light Pacifics'. 'Light' is a relative term of course!   *RCHS/Spence Collection*

The two nomenclatures were supposed to reflect the sections of the Southern where the engines were to work, but right from the start many WCs went to Kent and BBs to the West Country. Inevitably as time went on this distribution became even more disconnected.

Five months after the 70th engine appeared, and by this time in the ownership of the nation, the first of another 40 machines emerged, nos. 34071-110. These had the only significant modifications to the design, the replacement of the 8' 6" wide cab by a 9' wide one.

The first 19 of these were BBs and the 20th was given a one-off nameplate and name, as it was named for the last Chairman of the Southern Railway, Sir Eustace Missenden and allocated to the BB class (it also sported the only instance of green wheels and looked somewhat garish). The next 18 were WCs once again and the last two BBs, the very last one being completed some 8 months after its predecessor, pending modifications which never materialised, and it was the only BB without a squadron badge. (Another irrelevance here, this engine was originally going to be named 'Reginald Mitchell' to commemorate the designer of the Spitfires, a rather sad missed opportunity. Another 'lost' name was 'Hell Fire Corner'!). During this last production run the shape of some deflectors changed subtly, some (there doesn't seem to be a definitive list) being flatter than others. Nos, 34091 to 34110 were built with circular sandbox fillers which were capped by hinged circular covers, which usually hung loose. They all soon received the standard square fillers covered by sliding square covers. All locomotives were built with small fairings between the buffer beam and the front of the cylinders, but these were removed progressively through the early 1950s.

The narrow-cab 70 had 4,500 gallon tenders, 8' 6" wide, to give them route availability to include the Hastings line, but they never worked on it. Thus the final 40 had 5,500 gallon tenders 9' wide to match the cabs.

A very brief change in appearance occurred to 34004/5/6 in 1948 as they were chosen as Southern representatives in the mixed traffic category (Bulleid vindicated once again) in the Great Locomotive Exchanges of that year when they were fitted with extra long deflectors and the new cabs, both of which they retained afterwards, and were attached to LMS Black 5 tenders for the duration of the Exchanges, in which they excelled in everything except their fuel and water consumption. The Exchanges saw them working on the Great Central main line, ex-LMS routes along the Midland's Manchester main line and over the old Highland main line in Scotland and on the GWR from Bristol to Plymouth. Hornby have modelled 'Bude' in this condition. After 1951 four of the Bournemouth WCs, 34041 to 44, were regularly allocated to the S&D during the summer months, for which they were fitted with Whitaker token exchange apparatus on the tenders. Other members of the class made regular appearances on the S&D thereafter, as did the Rebuilds, well into the Western control period from 1958.

Other changes started to become apparent even before the class was complete. The first was the alteration to the shape of the cab by angling the front look-out windows to give the crew a wider angle of view, applied to locomotives from 21C164 onwards from new, together with three side windows each side instead of two. The earlier engines were then altered as they became due for General Overhauls, but it was a long drawn-out process, the last cab alteration taking place on 34015 in March 1957, just over a year after the first MN was rebuilt and only two months before the first Rebuilt Light Pacific emerged.

The next modifications affected the appearance of the 'flat tops'. At the front a cowl was added behind the

The only difference between 34099 and 34073 on the opposite page is the nameplate - this is a 'West Country', emphasising the point that this is really one class of engine. Although the MNs were really mixed traffic machines, BR classified them as 8P, indicating that they were regarded by BR as express passenger engines, but the LPs were classed as 6P5F and later 7P5F, thus recognising their mixed traffic role. 'Lundy' is leaving Salisbury on 11 March 1961.
RCTS CH00949

chimney which streamlined the look and hid the stovepipe effect of the massive outlet for the multiple exhaust. Then the safety valves, 3 of which were positioned in front of the dome, were replaced by two behind the dome on the shoulder of the boiler. These alterations took place between 1952 and 1956.

In 1952 three locomotives, 34011/43/65, together with 3 MNs received a series of alterations to try to correct some of the (very many) problems with the classes, in addition to those detailed above. Most obvious was the cutting down of the tender 'raves' to make access for coaling and watering much easier. These tenders were painted down to the running plates and the locomotive cabsides were also painted right to the bottom, giving a very different appearance to the later, and better-known, livery worn by other engines whose tenders were cut down from 1958, which kept the black panels on the lower part of the cab sides.

This is one of the three 1952 'tender rebuilds', 34011 'Tavistock', at Bournemouth on 8 September 1957, just after its GO in August that year. It now sports the final livery and condition of the class, except that the lion on the tender faces forward! The only Spamcans that sported the right-facing lion on a cut-down tender were the three 1952 engines, and only 34045 sported it on one with raves.
RCTS JAY2461

involved the positioning of a battery box on the flat plate above the front buffer beam, and speed recorders which were run from an eccentric on the left-hand rear driving wheel.

Major changes to the appearance of three locomotives involved experimental smoke clearance modifications to 34035/49 in 1959 during the pause in the rebuilding programme and the fitting of a Giesl Ejector to 34064 in May 1962, which made the locomotive's performance the equivalent of a Merchant Navy. One engine which stood out in the last years was 34006 'Bude' which retained its extra-long deflectors to the end, the other two Exchange engines being the eleventh and first Rebuilds respectively. 'Bude' worked the official Farewell to the S&D, double-heading with 'Biggin Hill' both ways along the full length of the line on 5th March 1966. Also in the last days, many ran with the sliding hatches, designed to

Only 60 locomotives were rebuilt, leaving 50 of the class unchanged to finish their working lives in the form that Bulleid designed. The subtle changes continued: as mentioned above, from 1958 until 1962 locomotives undergoing a General Overhaul had their tenders modified by cutting down the raves, although one 5,500 gallon and four 4,500 gallon tenders (the former always attached to 34078) went to the scrap yard with their raves intact. When the first 35 Rebuilds were undertaken the cabs were widened to 9' and the 5,500 gallon tenders from 35 of the last 40 locomotives were swapped with the narrow 4,500 tenders from the locomotives rebuilt, as a result of which there were a number of mismatched locomotive and tender combinations from 1957 onwards. From 1959 locomotives were fitted with BR AWS gear, which

cover things such as clack valves, open to reveal those parts.

For once there is little need to describe where they worked: where they didn't is probably more relevant. They didn't work over suburban branches in the normal course of events (although one can't say they *never* did), nor on the Lyme Regis branch or the Hayling line or the various light railways. Otherwise they went almost anywhere (except, as mentioned above, on the Hastings main line) and no post-War Southern layout is complete without one, or more. Hornby have done us a great service by producing a series of models which cover all of the common forms in which they worked.

Light Pacifics in the 1950s and 60s. 'Torrington' at the top is in early 1950s condition with the later 'V' cab and BR livery but otherwise as built whilst 'Lapford' is in final form with a cut-down tender (one of just five Originals to keep its 5,500 gallon tender), speedometer and BR AWS equipment. Hornby have accurately modelled the quite subtle changes to the locomotives as well as portraying the wider cabs and tenders of the last 40 engines. Modellers aiming to accurately reproduce a particular period should be aware of these changes to ensure they are buying models which would have worked alongside each other at any one time. Both: RCHS/Spence Collection

Opposite bottom - *Here we have (the inevitable) Rebuilt Light Pacific on a freight train, actually an engineers' train at Beaulieu Road on 5 March 1961* RCTS CH0940

Hornby have also produced fine models of the Rebuilt Light Pacifics, in most of their forms. As mentioned above, the early Rebuilds (which commenced in 1957) received wide tenders from 35 of the last 40 built. As there were 60 rebuilds that indicates that there should have been 25 which had mismatched wide cabs and narrow tenders. However, a few tender tanks were found to be wasted when being rebuilt and four new tanks, of 5,250 gallon capacity, were fitted, these

Right - Another tender variation, this time on a Rebuild. It is one of the BR-built 5,250 gallon tanks fitted to original underframes, all attached to Rebuilds. 34059 'Sir Archibald Sinclair' had this one from rebuilding until withdrawal. The most notable features were the lack of a 'step' in the top of the tank, enclosed vacuum cylinders and a single ladder on the rear. The train is seen at St James' Park Halt climbing up away from Exeter Central. Interestingly, the first coach seems to be a WR Autocoach - they were seen on Southern metals, at Seaton with 14xx tanks, after the 1963 WR takeover west of Salisbury.

service as possible during the busiest traffic periods. That is why some of the earliest built locomotives escaped rebuilding whilst some of the newest were rebuilt. For example, 34015 had a General in January 1957 and the next locomotive in, 34005, became the first rebuild; 34020 wasn't rebuilt but 34104, in for a General three weeks earlier in 1961, was. After the initial allocations to the Eastern Division the rest of the Rebuilds were shedded at most major depots across

being 9' wide, so only 21 Rebuilds were mismatches. The earliest Rebuilds were transferred to the Eastern Division in 1957 to cover the principal services until the Kent Coast electrification was completed. The first Rebuild, 34005, was run-in on Bournemouth trains for a short while before going east. The order of rebuilding seems at first glance to be totally random, but it was based on the requirement for General Overhauls and a limit of two locomotives in Eastleigh Works at a time for the first batch and four for the second batch. The timing was arranged to keep as many locomotives in

the Southern, appearing almost anywhere the Originals did with the notable exception of the Withered Arm lines to Bude and Wadebridge. They also worked all types of train, including the heavy ballast trains over the West of England main line from Meldon and in their last years were even to be seen working pick-up goods trains (I well recall seeing one shunting at New Milton one lunchtime).

Liveries for all the Light Pacifics were few even for the Originals, malachite green from new (they never sported wartime black) and then straight to BR Brunswick green throughout the nationalisation era. 34090 got a special version for its naming ceremony and seven got the experimental apple green livery for a time in 1948. Locomotives from 34091 onwards only ever sported Brunswick green, as did all the Rebuilds. Nameplate locations and the class 'ribbons' had various positions, some being especially positioned to accommodate the giant arrows for the 'Golden Arrow' service and some had special battons for the red 'Devon Belle' deflector-mounted 'wings'.

The last engine built, 34110, was one of the first to go, in 1963 when just 12 years old and the longest-lived Rebuild was 34013 which worked for nearly 10 years.

A final view (for now) of a Bulleid Pacific. This is 34010 'Sidmouth' on the Portsmouth Direct line with the 'Bournemouth Belle'. This shows us two things: the LPs did work the 'BB' and the 'BB' wasn't just to be seen on the Bournemouth road. During electrification in particular it would frequently be diverted, either via the Portsmouth Direct or the Mid-Hants line. On occasions in earlier times, if the main line across the New Forest was closed for some reason, Bournemouth expresses would be diverted via the 'Old Road' through Ringwood and Wimborne. Such diversions are manna for modellers!

<u>Bulleid Class Q1 0-6-0</u> (available in 4mm scale from Hornby)

Bulleid didn't have to make excuses for his second steam locomotive design - it was a goods (or freight) engine pure and simple and perfect for the austerity days of wartime. To say it looked unusual is like saying London is on the Thames, Bulleid saving weight wherever possible even to the extent of leaving off splashers and the running plate and using a strange geometry for the boiler cladding, the latter because the use of wartime insulating materials couldn't bear weight so an exoskeleton structure was needed. But they were very powerful and everything the Maunsell Qs weren't. 40 were built in two simultaneous batches at Ashford and Brighton in 1942 and numbered C1-40, in his strange coded system (I'm not explaining it here - it's been covered so often elsewhere). It was possibly this C which gave them their popular nickname of 'Charlies' which certainly indicates they were quite well liked. They were powerful and easy on maintenance for, despite their unconventional looks, they were simple inside cylinder 0-6-0s of the classic British

pattern with Stephenson valve gear and none of the sophisticated Bullied features of the Pacifics.

These engines had one Achilles heel - their braking power wasn't as good as the various 4-6-0s. However, with a fitted head they could haul a long goods train, and Feltham received the last 20 for such work. Although most Southern heavy freight ran at night there was also a considerable amount of daylight work, especially on van traffic and Inter-Regional transfer trains. These fell off sharply at the weekends when there was a parallel rise in the number of passenger extras and excursions, so the Q1s, like all Southern engines, saw some passenger work on such trains. The first 10 were allocated to Guildford and the next 10 to Eastleigh, from where one regular working took them down the West of England main line to Exeter on permanent way trains from Redbridge, a working which was later to be extended to Okehampton. Later allocations (around Nationalisation) included 10 at Tonbridge, from where they took over Hastings line goods work from the N1s and worked excursions at the weekend, and 5 to

Battersea, by which time they had received 'proper' numbers as 33001-40 of British Railways. The Battersea ones, and some later allocations to Gillingham, made them a common sight throughout the 'Garden of England' and they often worked through passenger trains on the Sheerness branch.

In 1953, following the North Kent floods, some were allocated to Faversham and Hither Green to help with the repairs but after that the allocations became 1 at Faversham, 4 at Norwood Jct, 1 at Hither Green, 12 at Tonbridge, 2 at Brighton, 1 at Nine Elms, 10 at Feltham, 6 at Guildford, and 3 at Eastleigh. Phase 1 of the Kent Coast electrification had little effect on them but after Phase 2 in 1962 most of the Kent machines went to Eastleigh and Guildford. In 1962 the Central Division received some for the first time, as a batch went to Three Bridges, just before withdrawals commenced in 1963 when 13 went, a process which was completed in January 1966, although 33006/20 were still at work a month after withdrawal and 33006 kept on until April!

As goods engines they were plain black throughout their lives, which makes renumbering the Hornby model easy. The only variation in their appearance was a lubricator driven off the front left hand axle, which was fitted from new to nos. 33029-40 and retrofitted to nos. 33001-4/6-10/3/2

'Charlie 1' as Bulleid first showed it to a no doubt astonished senior management of the Southern Railway in wartime. The plain black livery was highlighted by his 'sunshine' lettering but the positioning of the word 'Southern' on the tender doesn't seem to have made it into traffic, it reverting to the traditional position in the centre of the tank sides. 'Stark' hardly does it justice!
***Below** - From behind the engine still looks bizarre: the lack of a running board is said to have alarmed crews as they witnessed the coupling rods whizzing around just beneath their eye line. They soon got used to it!*

4 Modelling Ideas

In this chapter I'm going to take a break from locomotive matters and make a few suggestions about possible prototypes for models as well as to explore one or two 'what if' scenarios.

There's nothing quite like dreaming up your own history to justify the location of your model and, as you'll have gathered, one of the objectives of this work is to put forward a number of suggestions and scenarios to make that 'history' more plausible and thus to ensure that there are prototypical reasons for what you do with the railway.

Locomotives are probably the first items bought by modellers, so your locomotive stock tends to guide you towards certain types of railway scenario. If you have a large stud of Bulleid Pacifics, you will now know where they worked on the real railway, and when. Thus you will probably want to build a main line model but since most prototype locations require an enormous amount of space this is where the art of compromise and 'modellers' licence' comes in.

For example, one scenario is a secondary main line which is experiencing additional traffic due to a closure on the main line: engineering works, a breakdown, embankment slip or electrification might be the cause. This happened in the 1960s on the Alton to Winchester 'Watercress' line whilst the Bournemouth main line was 'juiced'. In fact, trains diverted that way had to be double-headed due to the severe gradients which had led to it being known as going 'over the Alps'. The 'Bournemouth Belle', all 12 Pullmans, was regularly seen on the line with a Bulleid Pacific and a pilot, sometimes a diesel for those who like to mix their motive power, on a single line route!

There are instances of towns which were 'missed out' by main lines due either to local politics or geography that militated against them in the early days. Shaftesbury is one such, and modellers' licence suggests that a later loop line might have been built from Semley via the town and back to the West of England main line at Gillingham. This would probably be single track and most stopping services would run via the loop. On the West of England route even these usually boasted larger engines, so the station would see quite a variety of locomotive types. Shaftesbury was an important town before the railways cut it off, so a railway loop might well have reinstated its position and even the ACE might have appeared here.

Another 'what if' scenario is a railway that was promoted but failed to be built. One such was a line from the Brighton main line just south of the famous Ouse Viaduct at Balcome, striking south east to Lindfield and Sheffield Park before terminating at Uckfield. It was actually started, in 1867, but abandoned before any permanent way was laid. If it had been completed the Bluebell Line would not have been built. As a model it would boast similar traffic to that of the Bluebell but might have seen more through trains to Lewes from the Brighton main line.

A further scenario is to postulate what might have taken place if an unsuccessful line was successful. In Kent there were a number of places where the railway companies tried to create new resorts, usually without success. But perhaps in a parallel universe the branch to Allhallows-on-Sea was electrified by the Southern before the War and became a very select resort in the 1950s. Electric commuter trains would have run, possibly using 4-CEP units and holiday extras would have seen plenty of steam action.

Similarly, Bexhill West was a disaster in terms of what the South Eastern Railway expected of it, but a modeller could make it that success and run more through trains and holiday extras to a station which could be modelled very much as it actually was, which could handle much more traffic than happened in reality.

One large area on the South Coast which was served only by branch lines is what is known today as the 'Jurassic Coast'. If just one shareholder at a meeting of the LSWR in the 1850s had voted for instead of against a motion to promote a railway, then a main line from Dorchester via Bridport to Exeter would have been built instead of the Yeovil to Exeter line. The possibilities of such a line are almost endless. Going against the lie of the land it would have twisted and turned to use valleys, would have had severe gradients and no doubt a tunnel or two. Bridport might have been a junction for a branch to Beaminster and West Bay might have become a more successful harbour. The line might have been either double or single track, the latter if the Yeovil line had also been completed (it was nominally an independent concern) and proven a tough competitor.

There are many different scenarios for the modeller and over the next few pages I have illustrated some further ideas which might encourage the thought processes.

Modelling ideas 1:
Bordon

As a possible terminus with variety in operation - and a bit of unusual colour in BR days - the LSWR station at Bordon would fit neatly into a limited space location. Here the camera has its back to the end of the line, whilst straight ahead the single line curves left towards Kingsley Halt and the junction with the main line at Bentley. The ground level LSWR signal box is slightly unusual in its frontal design whilst in the near distance the M7, No. 30027, stands alongside the open air coal stage and equally open air engine shed (another unusual prototype!). A single goods siding ran round the back of the right hand platform - a left hand platform once existed but was cut back at some stage leaving the left hand line to be used as part of the run-round loop. What makes Bordon so interesting however, was the presence of the Longmoor Military Railway whose own platforms and sidings were to the right, hence the bracket home signals on the approach. From Bordon LMR, trains would leave for Longmoor itself whilst there was also considerable interchange of traffic. M7s handled most of the branch traffic whilst the LMR would produce 'Austerity' tanks, a variety of superannuated former main line engines, and very old carriages. Of course, here is a branch line location where even 2-10-0s could appear - on the LMR. Another notable feature was the immaculate appearance of the Army engines - no need to weather *them*!

Norman Simmons, 19 April 1957

Further reading:
Branch Lines to Longmoor - Middleton Press
The Bordon Branch - written and published by Peter Harding
Track Layout Diagrams of the SR, Section S7, North Hampshire - G A Pryer and A V Paul.

Modelling ideas 2:
Norwood Junction

As an example of 'adapting the prototype' Norwood Junction loco might fit the bill. London area stations and locations are normally avoided by modellers due to their sheer size, but this wasn't massive, despite the neighbouring marshalling yards. If locomotives are your primary interest, the layout of the shed here affords possibilities with the potential for the passage of through trains, steam and electric, alongside. Dating from 1935, it was a five road dead-end shed with a 65' turntable out of sight at the end of the sidings that run between the shed and coaling stage. The main line from London Bridge runs immediately left of the coaling stage whilst on the right is the connection from the Norwood - Beckenham line to the aforementioned main line, both of which could be 'toned down' for a model. If you were to model it prototypically, it was home to the rare W class 2-6-4Ts, many elderly Brighton tanks, the three Maunsell Diesel Shunters and even the solitary Diesel prototype no 10800, the LMS-designed 800hp machine that no-one liked but which became the prototype of BR classes 15 and 16. The steam allocation was in excess of 40 locomotives, mostly freight types but that should not preclude any number of visiting engines, both Southern and from elsewhere.

Norman Simmons, 13 July 1957

Further reading:

An Historical Survey of Southern Sheds - OPC (This has the track layout plan)
Shed by Shed Part 5, Southern - St Petroc.

Modelling ideas 3:
DEMUs

If modelling the Southern Region from circa 1957 onwards there is no excuse for not including a DEMU (or several). Introduced firstly as six coach trains on the Hastings line, and then as two or three cars sets for other services, they were effectively a standard BR emu design with an on-board generator in the form of a diesel engine. Local passenger services on lines not yet slated for electrification thus enjoyed similar accommodation as the electrified routes. The first were introduced to the Hampshire local services around Southampton so they became known as 'Hampshire' units. Subsequent ones for the Salisbury to Reading services were known as 'Berkshire' units, detail differences in front end design and passenger accommodation applying between the various types. A 'Hampshire' DEMU model has been commissioned by the Cornish retailer Kernow Models from Bachmann. The trains were originally built with just two cars but later Nos. 1101-1118 and 1123-1133 were strengthened (or built) with three cars: 1114 is seen at Swaythling in its original two-car form. The first livery change came shortly after the view was taken with the provision of a yellow/orange 'V' at the motor coach end to indicate the presence of the guards/luggage compartment at that end of the train. The sets also survived well, being repainted variously over the years with yellow panel/full yellow end, all over blue blue/grey and a myriad of colours in the NSE and privatisation eras. With the availability of DCC sound, the characteristic sound of these machines may be faithfully recorded. Apart from west of Salisbury and to a greater extend on the Kentish main lines, they were rare, but otherwise their use was also widespread and eventually encompassed most of the non-electrified mainland branches as well as forees along the main line on the basis of through workings - the lack of corridor accommodation and thus lavatory access was not necessarily popular with passengers.

Modelling ideas 4:
Mixed stock

A 'different' train. Boat trains were renowned for a variety of stock whilst similarly their length could vary considerably. If you are looking for an excuse to mix maroon, green and Pullman then this could be the example. (Not sure if anyone produces the colourful headboards yet.) No. 34004 'Yeovil' is seen heading an up boat train from Southampton to Waterloo, full-brake vehicles for luggage, three Bulleid coaches for lesser mortals and four Pullmans for first-class. The combinations would vary almost train by train, the stock make up being shown in the special traffic notice, but there was certainly no set formation - hence the potential available. In the down direction the Pullman vehicles were usually at the rear: it saved those first-class feet having to walk too far down the platform at Waterloo. As an aside, pre-war and for a time during WW2 there was a short, fast service from Poole to Victoria behind a T9 with usually just three coaches, one of which was a Pullman. This particular train for the flying-boat service from Poole has been offered as a set by Hornby. The location above is Stoneham sidings south of Eastleigh. Black and white illustrations have appeared of at least one locomotive carrying an 'Ocean Liner' headboard running light and another on a freight working but still with the train headboard on the front. The engines concerned were in the process of returning to the home depot at Eastleigh, which was responsible for all supplying all Southampton Docks locomotives.

Further reading:

Excellent colour images of the headboards from the period can be found in any number of southern colour volumes, notably including (of course!), Waterloo to Southampton by Steam - Noodle Books

Modelling ideas 5:
Something different

continuing on from the previous page, a rather cruel enlargement of another colourful headboard, (there was more than one example of each) as well as a good illustration of the everyday 'look' of locos in the last days of steam. Even the headboard seems to have succumbed to the all-pervasive 'weathering'!

An excuse for anything. Now that the little railbuses are receiving attention from the RTR makers, how about this: an AC 4-wheel Railbus (either 79975 or 6) was recorded at Yeovil Junction whilst working the shuttle to Yeovil Town in the mid 1960s after 'Westernisation'. Two of them worked from 28 December 1964 until closure of Town station on 3 October 1966. Similar vehicles could be seen at Bodmin where a halt, known as 'Boscarne Exchange Platform', opened at Boscarne Junction on 15 June 1964 to serve residual traffic on the line to Bodmin North until its demise on 18 April 1966.

Bill White

Modelling ideas 6:
Modellers' licence

As mentioned in the text, attempting to follow or model a specific prototype can be difficult, if not actually impossible, notwithstanding the space available both in terms of room and wallet size. Consequently most will effect some form of compromise, whether that be as regards the layout design, stock used, or trains operated. The 'main' station at Ventnor Town on the Isle of Wight is well-known, but here we have Ventnor West, which if modelled prototypically, would limit locomotives to 02s, A1X Terriers and, perhaps, E1s and 3-4 trains a day including the only pull-push services on the Island at one time (leaving plenty of time for gardening/decorating/daydreaming etc). However if the last named are not a priority you might wish to consider this location at least as the basis for an interesting model. Clearly a terminus, I am not aware there were any plans to extend the line beyond the end seen, and anyway, geographically this would have been challenging to say the least. To the left, behind the trees, is a steep escarpment, along the bottom of which ran this branch from Merstone on the Newport to Shanklin line - a perfect backscene.

If you want more motive power variety, there were several attempts at a cross-Solent tunnel.....! Through trains might then be interspersed with excursions as well as the more typical branch workings. (Both Terrier and 02 types are either available or likely to be in the foreseeable future).

This early BR scene shows rather more carriages here than usual, the two crimson ones seemingly ex-works. The 02's oval numberplate can be seen on the bunker, with its number also still on the bufferbeam, a traditional display of identity which survived to the end of steam on the Island in 1966.

Further reading:: The Ventnor West Branch - Wild Swan. The Ventnor West Branch - written and published by Peter Harding. Memories of Isle of Wight Railways - Noodle Books

Modelling ideas 7:
Tank engines

It is of course always tempting to model the big engines, but remember the Southern had tank engines galore whose origins too were from all three constituent companies. At Brighton we see Terrier No. 32636 and E6 No. 32418, both suitably clean for enthusiast duty. You'll have to scratch or kit-build the E6, as the 'Terrier' is the only Brighton prototype modelled by the RTR manufacturers.

Whilst a Terrier and conceivably an E6 might well be seen in a variety of Southern locations, the same cannot be said for the Adams Radial tank. Usually constrained to the Lyme Regis branch, their only other wanderings were depot/works to Exmouth Junction and Eastleigh, and in their final years, on enthusiast specials to the western side of the London suburban area, the latter a return to the haunts they had worked when new. In many respects such limited operation was a pity, they were graceful engines whose styling clearly dates back to the Victorian era. Probably because of these limitations there is no ready to run model available, but we can always hope.

Modelling ideas 8:
The Leader

Rather than show the prototype, most of whose photos have appeared before, I thought this rather magnificent model would be appropriate. Every railway has its 'one-offs' and for the Southern that has to be No. 36001. (If you do not know what it is I doubt you should be reading this . . .). The model, made as a one-off' commission in 7mm, runs faultlessly - far better than the prototype ever did - and yes, it DID appear in black, albeit for just one day! (The layout is that of the builder).

The story of this intriguing design is the stuff of Southern legend (and a number of books by our publisher, Kevin Robertson!) and this very modern-looking machine was Bulleid's answer to the ongoing problem of a replacement for all the smaller tank engines inherited from the constituent companies. It started off as a simple tank engine design but Bulleid kept tinkering with it until this elaborate version was passed for construction. Just imagine the 'what-if' scenario envisaged by Bulleid, with hundreds of these machines replacing M7s, Hs and D1s! There is a project to release a RTR model in 4mm scale but it will have a long gestation period!

Modelling ideas 9:
Building Plans

What could be better than original railway company plans on which to base one's models? Here we see some examples: plans for a new house (for the Station Master?) at Chandlers Ford, and the design of the smallest Engine Shed on the Southern, built for one of

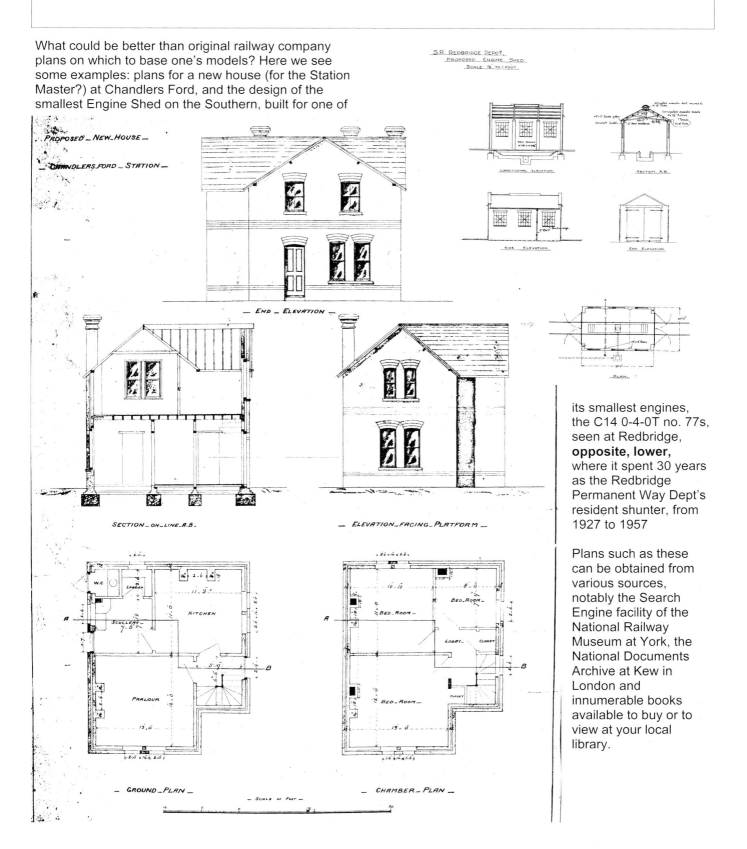

its smallest engines, the C14 0-4-0T no. 77s, seen at Redbridge, **opposite, lower,** where it spent 30 years as the Redbridge Permanent Way Dept's resident shunter, from 1927 to 1957

Plans such as these can be obtained from various sources, notably the Search Engine facility of the National Railway Museum at York, the National Documents Archive at Kew in London and innumerable books available to buy or to view at your local library.

Modelling ideas 10:
Sidings and Track Plans

Railway company track plans give the modeller a great deal of useful information. Not only does the plan below tell us that the LSWR was to put in some sidings at Dunbridge station at the behest of the War Department (dating this to 1915 or so) but it also shows the diversion of the roadway alongside the station. The sidings are described by their wagon capacity rather than their length, the radii of the curves are shown and the positions of signals are clearly marked out. The suggestion of a tramway in the notes is intruiging, although there is no sign of it on the plans!

The provision of a new pair of sidings for the Bursledon Brick & Tile Company also shows us how new customers would be treated. It doesn't indicate who has to pay the extortionist price though! Was it ever installed? The handwritten note says 'not carried out'.

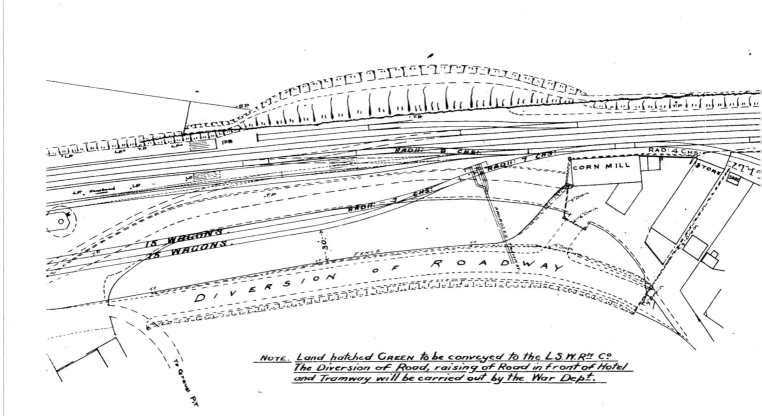

L. S. W. R.   DUNBRIDGE STATION

Proposed Alterations.

Scale 40 feet to an Inch.

NOTE. Land hatched GREEN to be conveyed to the L.S.W.Rⁿ Cᵒ
The Diversion of Road, raising of Road in front of Hotel
and Tramway will be carried out by the War Dept.

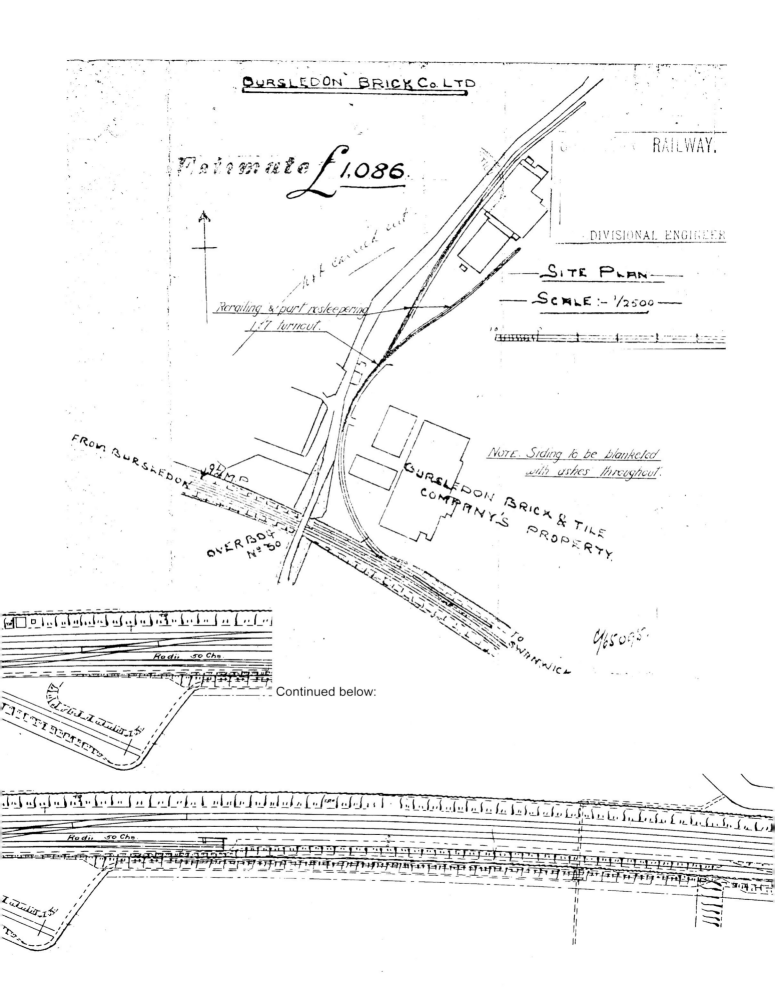

BURSLEDON BRICK Co LTD

Estimate £1,086.

RAILWAY.

DIVISIONAL ENGINEER

SITE PLAN

SCALE :- 1/2500

Rerailing & part resleepering
1:7 turnout.

FROM BURSLEDON

PUMP

OVERBOR No 30

BURSLEDON BRICK & TILE
COMPANY'S PROPERTY

NOTE. Siding to be blanketed
with ashes throughout.

TO SWANWICK

Radii 50 Chs.

Continued below:

Radii 50 Chs.

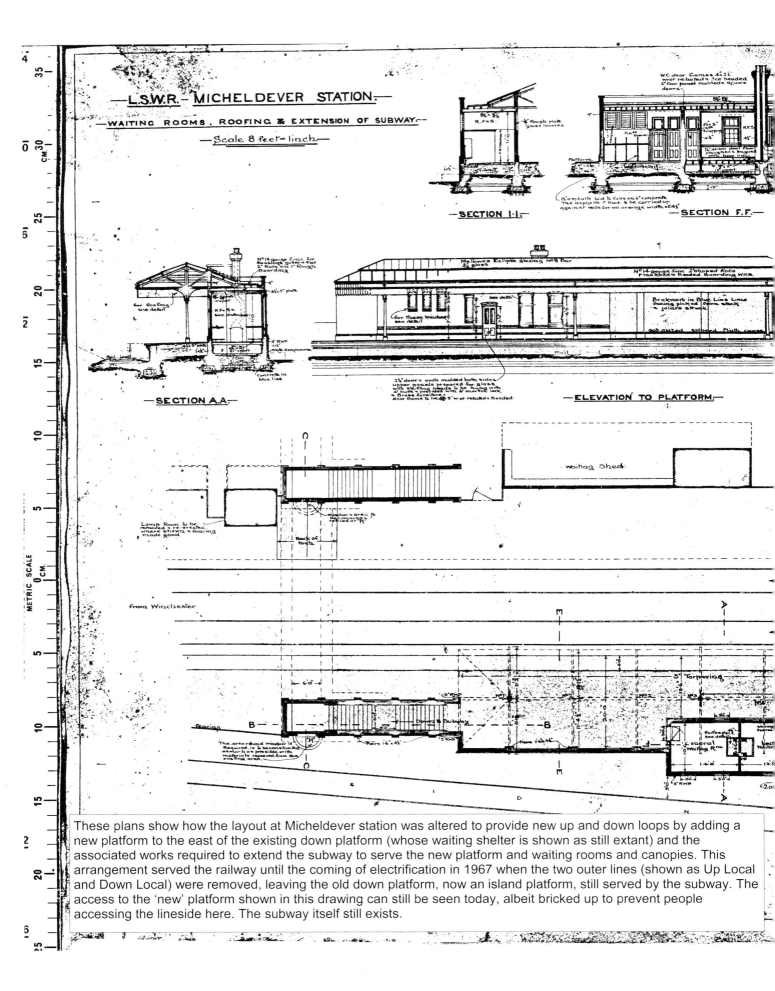

L.S.W.R. MICHELDEVER STATION.

WAITING ROOMS, ROOFING & EXTENSION OF SUBWAY.

Scale 8 feet = 1 inch.

— SECTION I.I. —

— SECTION F.F. —

— SECTION A.A. —

— ELEVATION TO PLATFORM. —

from Winchester

These plans show how the layout at Micheldever station was altered to provide new up and down loops by adding a new platform to the east of the existing down platform (whose waiting shelter is shown as still extant) and the associated works required to extend the subway to serve the new platform and waiting rooms and canopies. This arrangement served the railway until the coming of electrification in 1967 when the two outer lines (shown as Up Local and Down Local) were removed, leaving the old down platform, now an island platform, still served by the subway. The access to the 'new' platform shown in this drawing can still be seen today, albeit bricked up to prevent people accessing the lineside here. The subway itself still exists.

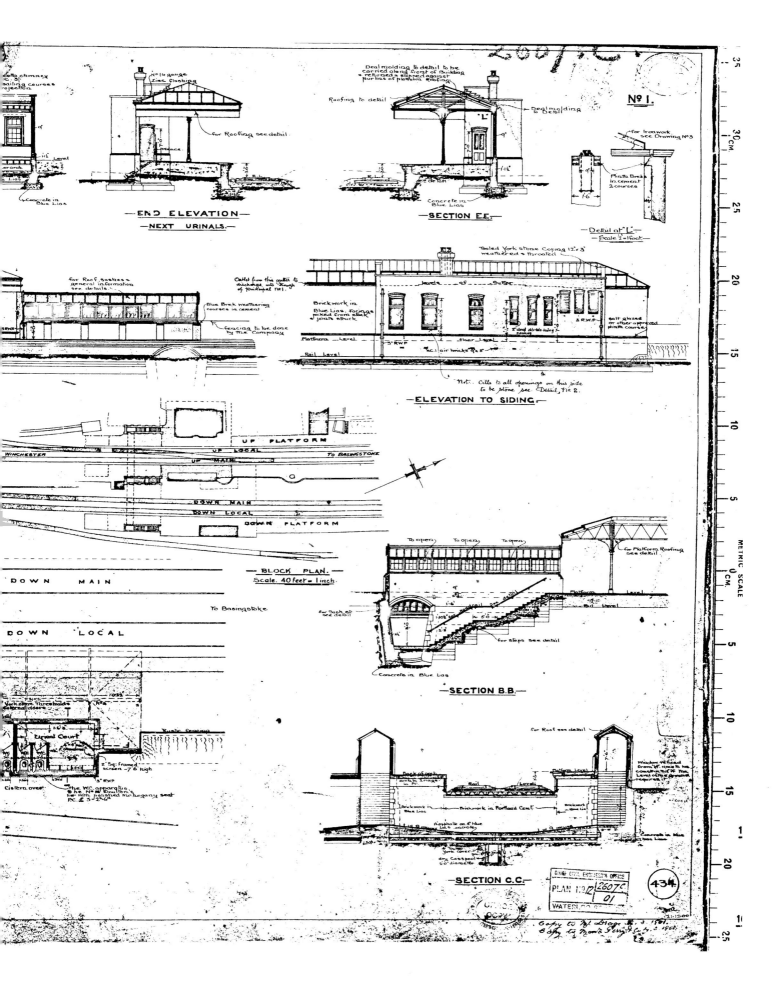

No 1.

Deal molding to detail to be
carried along front of Building
+ relturned + sloped against
purlins of platform roofing

Roofing to detail

Deal molding
to detail

"L"

for Ironwork
see Drawing No 3

Plinth Brick
in cement
2 courses

—SECTION E.E.—

—Detail at "L"—
—Scale ½=1 foot—

—END ELEVATION—
—NEXT URINALS.—

for Roofing see detail

Concrete in
Blue Lias

No 14 gauge
Zinc flashing

Concrete in
Blue Lias

Tooled York stone Coping 12"×3"
weathered + throated

for Roof sashes +
general information
see details

Outlet from this gutter to
discharge into trough
of handrail no 1.

Brickwork in
Blue Lias, facings
picked from stock
+ joints struck

Levels of Gutter

salt glazed
or other approved
plinth courses

Blue Brick weathering
courses in cement

fencing to be done
by the Company

Platform Level

Floor Level

Rail Level

3" RWP

Note. Cills to all openings on this side
to be stone see Detail No 2.

ELEVATION TO SIDING.—

UP PLATFORM

WINCHESTER

UP LOCAL

UP MAIN

TO BASINGSTOKE

DOWN MAIN

DOWN LOCAL

DOWN PLATFORM

— BLOCK PLAN. —
Scale. 40 feet = 1 inch.

To opers

To opers

To opers

for Platform Roofing
see detail

Platform Level

Rail Level

for steps see detail

for Soph. of
see detail

Concrete in Blue Lias

—SECTION B.B.—

DOWN MAIN

To Basingstoke

DOWN LOCAL

York stone Thresholds
external doors

External Court

Rustic fencing

2" Sq. framed
screen 7'6 high

Cistern over

3" RWP

The WC apparatus
to be Mr Doulton's
+ fitted with polished mahogany seat
PC £ 3-2'-6"

for Roof see detail

Platform Level

Rail Level

Brickwork in
Portland Cement

Brickwork in
Blue Lias

dry Cesspool
2'-0 diameter

—SECTION C.C.—

*A Drummond L11 heads for Eastleigh at Chandlers Ford station whilst **below** are the Victorian plans for alterations to the station. It was built on a line which opened on 1 March 1847, closed 5 May 1969 and, with completely new structures, reopened on 18 May 2003. Again, the cost estimates are fascinating!*

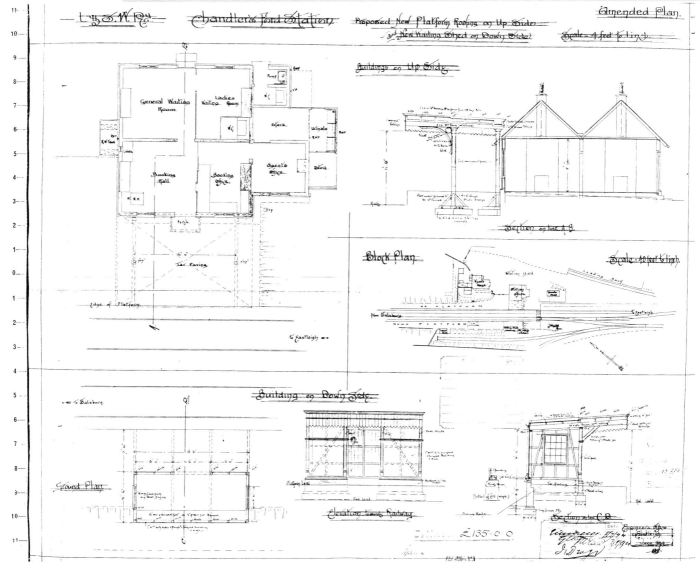

5 Passenger Trains

It's hardly a secret that the Southern was, to all intents and purposes, a passenger railway. Goods and freight traffic was its secondary consideration but still of vital importance to its profitability. You will have noticed a distinct lean towards the latter part of the Southern's business in this book so far and I am going to continue that theme.

However, it would be remiss of me to ignore the passenger business altogether, indeed, it would be unforgivable. But it is so important that it merits being a principal theme so that will be taken up in a future volume. For now I am going to outline the various types of Southern coaching without going into great detail about individual rolling stock histories or allocations and set formations, other than initial formations..

Passenger Trains

The term "carriage stock" includes vehicles without passenger carrying capacity, so herein we will refer to vehicles that do/did carry passengers as "coaches", although the two terms are often interchangeable. There was a considerable quantity of non-passenger carriage stock which still fell into the category. The Southern had an enormous passenger traffic and, although "comparisons are odious", it had around 1,000 more coaches than the GWR, which had a considerably greater route mileage. A large proportion of the Southern's passenger traffic was concentrated in the morning and afternoon "rush-hours" serving the great suburban sprawl around London.

A 'classic' view of a Southern passenger train, an express for the West Country headed by a Bulleid Pacific (35005 'Canadian Pacific'). At the head of the train is a Bulleid 3-car set, the most common arrangement, consisting of a BTK, CK and another BTK. Behind is a Maunsell BCK then another Bulleid set and further stock obscured by the smoke. The Maunsell BTK is probably destined for one of the Devon branches.   *RCHS/Spence Collection*

This commuter traffic and the services and rolling stock required to carry it had a profound effect on all the Southern's passenger traffic, since in its independent days the company was intent on electrifying as much of the system as possible, working outwards from the Capital. As a result, in much the same way as locomotive construction was affected, so was passenger rolling stock, and, once again, it was that nice man across the Channel who effectively derailed a well-planned re-equipment programme that led to a railway with many elderly and obsolescent coaches during the British Railways era. This, of course, is manna to enthusiasts as these are just the kind of things that cry out to be modelled!

On the Isle of Wight the impoverished constituent companies had relied on secondhand stock from the mainland, a policy continued by the Southern. 4-wheel coaches remained in daily use here well into Southern days. RCHS/Spence Collection

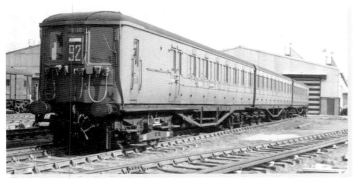

Southern suburban stock: a 3-Sub in its twilight days in service stock use. Early electric stock was based on pre-grouping designs (indeed, some sets consisted of converted pre-grouping stock) and fully panelled.

It has often been noticed that the Southern built no 'suburban' coaches and that the branch lines in the 1950s sported fascinating wood-panelled pre-grouping coaches. The reality is, of course, that it built *thousands* of suburban coaches but since they were formed into electric units they aren't usually 'seen' as such. Had World War 2 not happened, the wooden stock would probably have all been reduced to matchwood before the middle of the century and nice, clean electrics would have ruled the roost. The 'Southern Electric' is another major Southern story that will be expanded in great detail in a future volume.

Inherited coaching stock.

The Southern inherited large numbers of wooden stock from each of its constituents, most fitted with doors to every compartment. Each had built up extensive suburban networks and the LSWR and Brighton had commenced the electrification of these services with self-propelled electric traction rather than locomotive haulage.

This leads us on to a Southern speciality: coach 'sets'. Most of us are used to the concept of the Multiple Unit sets of the modern railway, but the Southern constituent companies had used this concept from Victorian days,

even for steam hauled coaches. Coaches were even ordered and built as sets, the SECR 'Birdcage' and LSWR 'Bogie Block' sets being particularly well known. Many of them were converted into electric stock by the Southern whilst others were converted to pull-push stock, so passengers in the suburbs and on country branches actually rode in internally-identical stock. Due to the desire to get as many commuters as possible seated this stock was quite cramped: the SECR achieved the greatest capacity with its 10 compartment third class coaches. In addition to stock allocated to sets there were numbers of unallocated 'loose' stock.

The distinctive guards' lookouts at the ends of the SECR 3 car sets were known as 'Birdcages', many surviving in service stock into the 1960s. David Chalmers

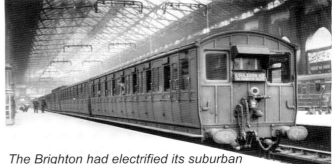

The Brighton had electrified its suburban services with overhead AC but the Southern standardised on 3rd rail DC. Some Brighton AC stock became steam-hauled p-p trains! RCHS/Spence Collection.

Main Line Corridor Stock

At Grouping there was an urgent need to build new main line corridor stock for express services as the three main constituent companies had only a very few up to date designs.

Pre-grouping corridor stock was similar to non-corridor in appearance, although the LSWR had produced some steel-clad designs after WW1 which were to form the basis of the earliest Southern stock introduced under Maunsell's regime. In 1923 there were four sets of them for Bournemouth services and two First Class versions for Southampton Ocean Liner Expresses. These coaches were known as the "Ironclad" stock and were the only reasonably modern stock acquired by the Southern, so the design was initially perpetuated for new construction, as was their livery, lined-out dark green, which became the Southern standard. The LSWR also had around 250 pre-war wooden corridor stock, generally similar to its late-Victorian stock.

The SECR had just 21 gangwayed corridor coaches - 15 Birdcage Brake Composites and 6 Thirds, used on through trains to other railways although it also had a single set of 8 'Continental' coaches built for the boat expresses. More of the latter were ordered as the need for more Boat train stock was desperate. These coaches had distinctive vertical matchboarded sides.

The SECR's dearth of stock was also acutely felt on

The nearest thing the LBSC had to a modern design was its 'Balloon' stock, one of which is seen near the end of its days.
Colin Hall

the old LCDR lines to Thanet. A version of the 'Ironclad' design was produced, with a narrower profile to suit the restricted North Kent line clearances: this was known as 'Thanet' stock. The Southern ordered nine 8-coach sets plus 5 loose Composites in 1923. 'Continentals' and 'Thanets' lasted in service until the 1950s.

The Brighton had no corridor coaches and the Southern built no more coaches to LBSC designs. Like the SECR it had relied on the Pullman Car Company, based at Brighton, to provide catering facilities, usually a single Pullman Car in an express passenger train.

Maunsell Southern Designs

The 'Ironclad' design became a temporary Southern 'standard' coach: six more 5-coach sets and 26 loose coaches were already on order and Maunsell added a further four 5-coach and four 2-coach sets plus six more Dining Saloons. Finally two 11-coach sets were ordered for use on the Central Section's Brighton lines, one for the 'City Limited' and one for the Bognor line. These

Pre-Grouping wooden-bodied LSWR corridor stock is seen at Brockenhurst in 1953, now relegated to excursion or occasional use. A 'stranger' creeps in on the left . . . but we're interested in the coaches here*. The middle one displays the adherence to droplights opposite every compartment. The term 'corridor stock' doesn't necessarily mean coaches with gangways, some had internal corridors without connecting gangways to other stock.
*OK, for those who don't know, some V2s were lent to the Southern in 1953 when the MNs were temporarily grounded after 35020 broke its driving axle at Crewkerne. 'Strangers' will be detailed in Volume 2.   David Kimber

Behind the Maunsell Q 0-6-0 (built as a goods class!) is a set of Southern-built 'Ironclad' stock, set no. 472 being the rump of the 11-coach set built in 1926 for Bognor services reduced to 3 coaches. Note the distinctive turn in at the ends of the 6-comp't brake 3rds (nos. 4046/7), a characteristic of 'Ironclad' stock. Oxted, 1953.

latter emphasise the fact that complete train sets were ordered for specific services. Most 'Ironclad' stock lasted until the end of the 1950s (the 2-coach sets as pull-push sets from 1948) and then many went into service stock, as their name was as equally applicable to their strong construction as to the fact that they were the first steel-panelled Southern stock.

The urgent orders above were produced to deal with a crisis: Maunsell's first new design for the Southern didn't appear until 1926 and over the following decade 1,320 gangwayed corridor coaches were built for locomotive-hauled trains. They were divided into three 'periods', the first, comprising about one-fifth of the total, are known as 'low window', the next 700 or so are 'high window' and the final 20% the 1935/36 flush-sided designs. 46 catering cars of various types completed

the fleet. In addition there were variations to these designs, on longer underframes, for use in main line electric units for the Brighton, South Coast and Portsmouth electrification schemes.

The general Maunsell coach outline was quite handsome, although continuity of line was not a strong point. Variations in window height and general shape meant that even a set of coaches built as a set would look like a hotch-potch of designs. The nearest state of harmony was achieved in the early 'low window' period, when all windows were at least of the same height. The 'high window' period saw the height of the corridor-side windows raised virtually to the cantrail, but only the larger, fixed, windows. Thus no continuity of line was evident. Another oddity was the tumblehome, curved along the passenger accommodation but virtually flat-

The post-nationalisation Newhaven Boat Train well illustrates the 'hotch-potch' appearance of Maunsell's coaching designs. This was the first Southern set to receive the 'blood & custard' livery, the 'blood' being repeated above the window line, it was later amended to run just below the cantrail. The first coach is a 'Continental' brake 3rd. RCHS/Spence Collection (both photos on this page)

sided for guards' and luggage accommodation. Not that this bothers us as modellers! In fact, it gives a distinct variety in our models as Hornby have produced most of the common R4 designs of the low and high window periods. One variation which continued through the various periods virtually unchanged, the Open 3rd, scarcely matched *any* of its contemporary designs.

Due to narrow clearances on the North Kent line, around Lewes and on the Tonbridge to Hastings line there was the necessity to produce variants with a narrower profile than the standard 9' wide stock. The latter was designated Restriction 4 (R4), the Chatham and Lewes stock (8' 6" wide) Restriction 1 (R1) and the Hastings coaches were Restriction 0 (R0)*, the latter, at 8' 0¾" wide, able to 'go anywhere'. There were 102 R0 coaches built, all in the 'high window' period. They had virtually flat sides and no guards' duckets but were generally similar in layout to the wider coaches but seated just 2 across in 1st class and 3 across in 3rd (no 2nds were built).
* As a matter of interest R2 and R3 stock were pre-grouping profiles: Maunsell built no coaches to these restrictions.

The R1 stock was built with both low and high windows with a flat van profile without a ducket and a slightly wider passenger part with a shallow tumblehome. 175 of these were built, including 82 General Saloons.

Most modellers of 4mm scale layouts will be interested in the Maunsell R4 stock, since Hornby have produced vehicles to eight of these designs, in four liveries, six of which are available in both low and high window styles. The notable exceptions are catering vehicles and the General Saloons (R1).

Composites were mostly formed in sets whilst most all-1sts were used on Boat Train work, although some were used in high-profile set trains.

Most confusing are the Brake coaches. Three designs have appeared, 6-compartment Brake 3rds, 4-comp't Brake 3rds and 6-comp't Brake Composites. An additional Brake Composite to the last, 1936, design

has been released as a pull-push trailer and will no doubt appear in its original form at a later date. The other four designs are the Open 3rd, Corridor 3rd, Composite and all-1st, these last three available as low or high types as are the first three brake vehicles above.

The low window 4-comp't Brake 3rds were used at each end of a 3-car set with a Composite between them, two batches of which were built. The first batch, sets 390-9, were for West of England services and were transferred to the Somerset & Dorset line in the 1950s. Four more sets, 445-8, remained on the Southern. The long van space was a hangover from Edwardian times when families would travel with almost everything they owned but in the late 1920s the luggage requirement was reduced and only 27 4-comp't Brake 3rds were built with high windows.

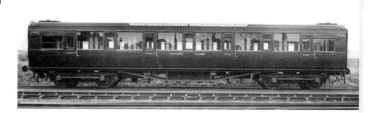

Maunsell's standard high window stock: at the top is an all-1st and below a Composite. The First (allocated to Southampton Ocean Liner Express duties) shows the extra height of the large fixed windows. The Composite shows the Bulleid 1938 livery for coaches allocated to the 'Bournemouth Limited' (progenitor to the Malachite Green standard livery), this one being used in Weymouth 3-set 221.   *Both: Dick Coombes*

S6570 was a Brake Composite with low windows. From the compartment side high and low stock looked identical. These coaches were introduced to serve the Devon branches as 'complete trains'. They would be formed in expresses, in particular the ACE, and detached at the branch junction to give these lines through services to Waterloo. Here it's seen at Ilfracombe formed in set 353.   *David Chalmers*

20 of the Maunsell 1935 Brake Composites and 20 1933 Open 3rds were converted to pull-push operation from 1959-61 to replace the early wooden bodies p-p units. Hornby produce this type of set and a standard, unconverted version of the Open 3rd. These sets were used across the Southern branches.   David Chalmers

There were just 4 low 6-comp't Brake 3rds (plus 2 identical Brake 2nds, later reclassified Brake 3rd - and finally back to 2nd) but this became the principal type of high window brake vehicle. There were 92 of them, mostly allocated to sets. The Brake Composites were built in both styles and were originally 'loose' stock to provide through services to the West of England branches, although many later ones were formed with the 6-comp't Brake 3rds to form 2-coach 'P-sets' for use on local services throughout the system.

Thirds came in two forms, Compartment or Open. The former matched the other coach styles but the Open 3rds, with doors only at each end, were the odd men out, having drop windows without ventilators. Some of them were paired with Restaurant/Kitchen Cars for use as Restaurant seating but most Thirds, of both types, were used as loose stock and when a Third was formed in a set, it was usually a Compartment 3rd.

The final Maunsell stock built in 1935/36 had the doors in the corridor side repositioned, flush-fitted windows (1935 stock only) and full-height fixed quarter lights

whilst the Open 3rds had windows with opening ventilators of differing types. Other types of these last Maunsell designs were Brake Composites, Brake 3rds, Corridor 3rds and 1st/3rd Composites. The Brakes all had 6 compartments.

The Maunsell catering vehicle story is extremely complex as many were rebuilt to various different layouts after WW2. The only way to create one appears to be to use after-market sides on a Hornby chassis or bespoke chassis. Hopefully Hornby will produce an RTR one to go with their superb range!

Bulleid Southern Designs

Bulleid started by re-liverying Maunsell coaches but the approach of war somewhat hampered him in the production of new designs. His first batch of passenger vehicles appeared in 1946, on underframes built in 1940. Consequently these eighteen 3-coach sets had 'short' 59' underframes, all other Bulleid stock using new frames of 63' 5" length. These eighteen sets plus four on the longer frames adopted the Maunsell pattern

Bulleid's 'Lyme Regis' heads a West of England train in which the first three coaches are of the multi-door style built on 59' underframes, set numbers 963-80. Both engine and coaches appeared in the same year, a further batch of similar coaches appearing in 1946 as sets 981-4 on the new standard longer 63' 5" underframe. The rest of the train consists of Maunsell stock.

RCHS/Spence Collection

of doors to each compartment and were the only Bulleid stock to have these. All were allocated to WoE duties until 1959 when the first ten of the short-frame series were sent to the Somerset & Dorset to replace the Maunsell low window sets..

All Bulleid's stock had smaller van sections than had gone before, without the odd width, giving a far more pleasing appearance. Similarly window heights were standard along the train. Look-out duckets were superseded by roof-mounted periscopes. The first ones ordered were built by the Birmingham Railway Carriage & Wagon Company (BRCW) but delivery was delayed

so Eastleigh stock ordered a year later appeared first. The BRCW stock differed to the Eastleigh stock in a number of ways as the company used its own construction methods: most noticeable were the windows, which were 3" shallower. Only Brake 3rds and Composites were built by BRCW, all formed into 3-coach sets, the first ten known as Type M and the later twenty-five Type L.

Type L also applied to the first Eastleigh built 3-coach sets, nos. 770-93, which had 10½" (shallow) sliding ventilators. The Brake 3rds had two compartments and a 32 seat open saloon, the composites being all

Set s801 was one of the ten 'Cross-Country' sets built by BRCW for services to Dover, Ramsgate and Margate. They differed to the remaining 25 sets by having a coupe compartment next to the brake van and seating for 44 rather than 48 passengers. They had shallow sliding vents and box-type rooftop vents. RCHS/ Spence Coll.

compartment stock. This would become the most common formation of Bulleid coaching stock.

Following the 3-sets a batch of eleven 6-coach sets (nos. 290-300) were built for Bournemouth line services. These had extended sides covering the solebars and unique Restaurant and Kitchen cars as well as the only shallow-vent Open 3rds. They were regarded as some of the finest coaches of their time and appeared in 1947, the last sets to include catering vehicles as part of their make-up.

The only other shallow-vent sets were 2-coach sets Type R (sets 63-75) which had a Brake 3rd and Brake Composite for use on branches and the West of England line, although in practice they only worked on the WoE. There were also 45 loose Composite Brakes for WoE branch through trains. Finally there were 13 loose Corridor Composites and 5 Corridor 3rds. We'll come back to the catering stock shortly.

The remaining Bulleid coaches had deeper (15" deep) sliding ventilators. These are probably of most interest to modellers as the Bachmann releases are of this stock, the first of which was a batch of fifteen 4-coach sets for Eastern Section services (sets 80-94) which

Bulleid was keen on labour-saving ideas and introduced carriage washing plants, which he claimed could also be used for his Pacifics (there's no evidence this actually happened). His coaches had flush sides and above we see one of the Bournemouth 6-coach sets receiving the treatment, possibly at Clapham Jct. RCHS/Spence Coll.

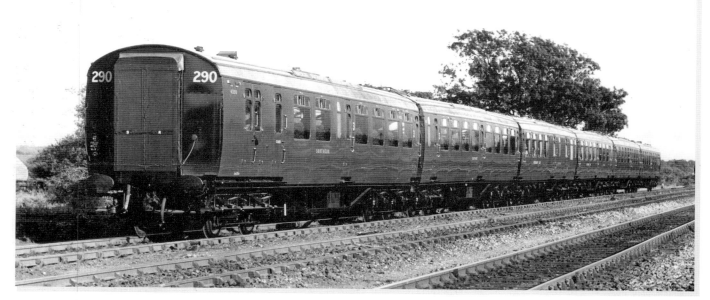

The celebrated Bulleid 6-coach sets nos 290-300 produced specifically for the principal Bournemouth line expresses were possibly his finest creation. Universally liked, they incorporated many modern features and were considered to be superior in most respects to the BR Standard mk 1 coaches that later supplemented but never supplanted them.
RCHS/Spence Collection

incorporated a corridor 3rd in the formation; otherwise they were the same as the 3-sets. These Type N sets can be accurately made up from Bachmann models.

The Type Ns were followed by more Type L sets (830-49) with the new deep vents, although the last 12 were

immediately upgraded to 5 coach sets by the addition of two Compartment 3rds and the others would receive a pair each summer. These sets can also be made up from Bachmann models. At the same time 40 Corridor 1sts were built for Boat Train use but not allocated to sets. 40 Corridor 3rds were also loose stock.

A Bulleid type N 4-coach set with deep vents stands in Brighton station behind Southern-allocated Ivatt class 2 tank no. 41327. Set 86 was one of 15 sets which were the last to be introduced to traffic in a green livery. In the background is a Maunsell electric set from the late 1930s with flush window panels.
Mark Abbott

The final Bulleid sets (850-65) had coaches with long roof-top water tank covers and were Type L 3-sets. These can't be accurately represented by Bachmann models but that's of little consequence as the earlier ones can! A batch of 45 Open 3rds were built for Boat Train work - plus a solitary Corridor 1st - and a number of Corridor 3rds which would be added to the sets in pairs for the Summer timetables.

Bulleid Catering Stock

Despite its not being available RTR the Bulleid catering stock needs little introduction. These are the famous 'Tavern Car' pairs, made up from a Kitchen & Buttery Car (the Tavern Car itself) and an Open Composite Restaurant Car (the Tavern Trailer).

Controversy surrounded them from the start. Bulleid had intended to encourage diners or drinkers not to dally too long in these vehicles and in that respect they were an overwhelming success! However, that was because the passengers hated them as Bulleid had provided only toplights instead of 'proper' windows. Almost immediately the Trailers were withdrawn and fitted with nine normal windows each side which stopped the protests. They kept their faux 'brickwork' for only a few years and their painted-on Inn names through a change to green livery from 1957 until they were rebuilt as Kitchen/Buffet Cars with normal windows between June 1959 and June 1960.

Initially six pairs were sent to the Eastern and LM Regions but were soon returned to the Southern, where they worked on the West of England line. One pair was allocated to the 'Royal Wessex' from 1954 and another (7897 and 7838) was added to BRCW set 805 together with a BR mk1 Open Second no. 44230 in 1957 to create an additional 6-set for the Bournemouth line.

'Tavern Trailer' no. 7840, **top**, is seen as built with no 'proper' windows, paired with Tavern Car no. 7899 'At the sign of The Crown'. **Below:** it's seen a year or so later after being rebuilt although the only change to 7899 is to its name, which has now become 'At the sign of The George and Dragon'. These sets were used on West of England trains, normally marshalled at the London end of a train as they were removed from or added to trains at Exeter Central as shown here. It seems that a Bulleid Pacific is being used as station pilot on this occasion! The large windows in the Tavern Car light the corridor, the bar area remained gloomy until rebuilding in 1959/60
Dick Coombes(top)/Les Elsey.

Pullman Cars on the Southern

No account of Southern passenger stock would be complete without describing the Pullman Cars used for prestige services, even if they were independently owned and staffed.

The Southern was the country's biggest user of Pullman Cars, the Pullman company having its UK works at Brighton, Preston Park. In 1929 it used 141 out of 245 Pullman Cars in the UK, in 1939 147 out of 207, in 1946 145 out of 198, in 1955 141 out of 194 in 1960 119 out of 252 and in 1967 34 out of 143.

Pullman Cars (never coaches) were incorporated in electric sets, formed into special all-Pullman sets, used loose, used in boat trains, company trains and named trains. There were 12 wheeled and 8-wheeled Pullmans, parlour cars, kitchen cars, brake 3rds, brake 1sts and so on.

Both the SECR and Brighton used Pullmans in lieu of having their own catering vehicles, but the LSWR built 'Dining Saloons' and had no use for Pullmans. Dedicated all-Pullman trains were introduced by the Southern, promoted as prestige trains .Many of these trains started as Sundays only or summer only trains, including the famous 'Bournemouth' and 'Devon Belles'. The first was hugely successful and became daily, lasting until the end of steam, whilst the latter lasted just a few summer seasons. One outstanding train was the 'Brighton Belle', the only all-electric Pullman train in the World, which was really a prestige business train working twice each weekday from Brighton to London.

On the old SECR lines a number of Pullman trains ran

Top - *Pullmans were often used for special trains conveying important people such as Royalty or visiting Heads of State. The Southern kept a number of T9s in immaculate condition over the years for these duties. In the early days of flying a T9 was the regular power for Flying Boat Specials from Victoria to Poole.*

Main picture and inset- The 'Devon Belle' was introduced in 1947 to cover for a lack of serviceable passenger stock until the Bulleid programme got under way. It's most innovative feature was its Observation Car at the rear of the train, which ran to Ilfracombe. It slowly petered out, finishing service in 1955 after which the Observation Cars saw service on other parts of the BR system.   All: RCHS/Spence Collection

including the 'Thanet Belle, the only one of these 'Belles' to sport anything other than a Bulleid Pacific in the 1950s. Perhaps *the* prestige train of that decade was the 'Golden Arrow', the only train to receive the post-war all steel Pullman Cars built in 1951 and chosen as one of the 'Festival of Britain' trains. Its use of spotless 'Britannias' was the only long-term use of the BR Pacifics on the Southern.

The all-Pullman 'Golden Arrow' re-established the traditional Continental Boat Train services to France when it was reinstated on 15 April 1946 running from Victoria to Folkestone but returning from Dover. Bulleid's new Light Pacifics were its normal power until 1951 when the famous pair of 'Britannias' was sent to Stewarts Lane shed specifically for the "arrer".

Below - The Brighton line saw Pullmans with greater frequency than other Sections of the Southern, single Pullmans being part of the 37 6-PUL units and five making up each of 3 5-BEL all-Pullman units for the 'Brighton Belle' services.

All: RCHS/Spence Collection

Non Passenger Coaching Stock (NPCS)

This category includes all those vehicles which were passed to run in passenger trains without carrying passengers. This includes Special Cattle Vans, milk tankers, scenery and Post Office vans as well as the many purely luggage vans which are well known. Unlike other companies the Southern didn't use normal coach profiles for these but a cross between traffic vans and coaches. They had outside frames and planked sides and appeared in both 4- and 8-wheeled versions. Construction included even and uneven planking and a batch of plastic bodied 4-wheelers was built in 1943/4.

There were vans with and vans without guards' accommodation; curiously the only ones with such equipment

An up Ocean Liner Express heads past Eastleigh Airfield in the 1950s at Stoneham Sidings behind 'Lord Howe'. The first vehicle is a Gangwayed Bogie Luggage Van for passengers' luggage and the train is a heterogynous collection of Maunsell, Bulleid and BR stock. There's even a Pullman in there!

Les Elsey

A 'Hornby' heads a Newhaven Boat Train through Three Bridges with a pair of Luggage Vans (coded PMV by BR) at the front. These were the most numerous Southern NPCS vehicles, over 770 being built. The engine is 20003, the final one of three machines designed by Raworth and Bulleid as the prototype freight engines for a fully-electrified Southern. They were known colloquially as 'Hornbys'.
Paul Hersey

Right - A 'Van C' (BR type BY) as modelled by Hornby. 268 were built and they were to be seen across the system. 130 bogie versions were known as a 'Van B'.

Paul Hersey

were *non*-gangwayed! Hornby produce both the bogie Van B and 4-wheel Van C whilst Bachmann cover the 4-wheel Luggage Vans with PLV/PMV and Covcar/CCT variants, the latter having end doors similar to the BR GUVs.

None of the other Southern NCPS vehicles are produced as RTR models, other than the Hornby Gangwayed Bogie Luggage Van which is extremely long-in-the-tooth. We'll cover kits for them in another volume.

H15 'Chonker' 30487 rattles (or should that be 'chonks'?) along the South Western mainline with a long milk train from London. Milk tanks were considered to be non-passenger coaching stock and ran at passenger train speeds. The West of England milk train was normally the province of Bulleid Pacifics: the up service from Templecombe was hauled by the Merchant Navy pacific which had taken the celebrated ACE westwards earlier in the day. Of interest is the Maunsell Brake Composite in the middle for the guard. The train was fully fitted.
Ted Gamden

6 Goods Traffic

There is a common misconception that the Southern carried little freight, or goods, traffic. (The terms are interchangeable, but 'goods' seems to have been the favoured term in Victorian days whilst the present-day railway carries 'freight'. During the timescale covered in this book the use of the terms seemed to overlap so I have used both, although, being essentially 'steam age' myself, the use of 'goods' predominates).

What it carried was a different *mix* of goods, at different times to other railways.

So the modeller needs to understand how the Southern dealt with its goods traffic in order to plan his layout and, especially, the way the goods trains should interact with 'glamorous' express and local passenger trains.

Unlike the other parts of the country, there was little originating mineral traffic in the South of England. The northern railways were built up to handle the coal, iron and steel traffic which was the foundation of the Industrial Revolution, as was the Great Western in South Wales and the Midlands. Heavy industries in Scotland also generated much long-distance heavy mineral traffic for its (very different) railways. This traffic was highly visible on those lines but non existent on the Southern (except in the Kent coal field). However, if you subtract the mineral traffic there was still a great deal of 'other' freight traffic and the Southern handled virtually as much, pro-rata, as the bigger companies. All the same, it was always subsidiary to the passenger traffic, contributing less than a quarter of the company's revenue in the early 1930s. The corollary of this was

Hardly a typical Southern goods train, but this does continue the theme in this book by showing what is usually seen as a classic pure Express Passenger locomotive in the form of one of Maunsell's great 'Schools' class V 4-4-0s working hard with a fitted goods from the Southampton area up the long climb through the chalk at Micheldever in May 1961. 30913 'Christ's Hospital' is my favourite member of the class, named after my Father's school in Sussex, which had its own station! I wished it had been my school as well . . . RCTS CH01134

that the industrial downturn in that decade had less effect upon the Southern than it did on the others. The type of goods traffic carried is relevant to the types of locomotive a railway builds. Mineral traffic was usually slow because the wagons didn't have continuous brakes. Thus those companies handling such traffic had to build slow but powerful locomotives with good braking ability and all but the Southern built 2-8-0s and BR built 2-10-0s.

With no heavy mineral runs the Southern's biggest goods tender engines were 6-coupled and most were really mixed traffic engines. As we've seen, the various CMEs certainly considered 8-coupled goods engines but all came to the conclusion that they were unsuitable for Southern requirements. The use of ROD and WD 2-8-0s for brief periods of time after the two World Wars just served to confirm these opinions. During the day the ex SECR N moguls could haul local passenger trains and at night cross-London freights, as could the Brighton Ks and LSWR S15s. Curiously, the Southern's last "purely" goods engines were simple 0-6-0s, albeit with the Bulleid touch, his Q1 'Charlies' (and even they were to be seen on passenger trains at times).

As noted earlier the Southern was mainly a passenger carrier so most of the available paths on the main lines were devoted to such traffic. In steam days freights were much slower than passenger trains, so the Southern effectively separated the flows by running much of its freight traffic at night, when passenger traffic

The LSWR's best express locomotives, the 'Greyhound' T9s, weren't above getting their paws dirty on pick-up goods duties. High-stepping no. 30710 undertook such humble work on 19 May 52 at South Molton on the North Devon line.   *RCTS PHW0654*

was infrequent or non-existent. This had the added advantage that locomotives could be used on either type of traffic and accounts for the mixed traffic designation of many Southern locomotives, notably the Bulleid Pacifics. In fact, goods traffic was specifically banned during the morning and evening peaks in the London suburbs. By contrast, the further away from the suburbs one was the more likely it was that a goods train would run in daylight hours. This was for a number of reasons, the first being that there was less traffic and

An unidentified LBSCR class C2X heads the Midhurst pick up goods near Selham during the period when the branch catered for goods traffic only, between 7 February 1955 and 6 May 1963 when the line closed completely . The class was the standard Brighton goods type with the celebrated K moguls handling the heavier main line work. A model of a goods-only branch after the cessation of passenger services would make an unusual model.   *C Griffiths*

therefore there were more paths available at night. Another was that there were few 'lay-by' sidings for slow goods trains due to the separation of the traffic flows, the tendency being to provide running loops such as those at Waller's Ash on the South Western main line's climb up through the chalk north of Winchester. All the main lines had quadruple track within the reach of London, although this was primarily to separate the stopping passenger services from the expresses. It's noticeable that the Southern had 'local' and 'through' lines on quadruple sections whereas the LMS, for example, had 'passenger' and 'goods' lines.

Many branches and lines such as those on the 'Withered Arm' would close down at night. It followed that as the trunk route hauls ran at night, the feeder services had to run in the daytime to get the wagons in place before the trunk services could depart, or the distribution services couldn't depart until the overnight ones had arrived and been split and remarshalled. For example, on 16th April 1955 the 08.20 up Plymouth Friary to Exmouth Junction freight left Plymouth behind a pair of Light Pacifics, nos. 34057/8. We know this because the second engine caught fire (a common problem with the Spamcans in the mid 1950s) and had to be removed from the train at North Tawton.

From the modeller's perspective, there are two scenarios here - after all, a pair of Bulleids was as rare as hen's teeth on the Southern, let alone on a goods train, let alone on the system beyond Exeter, let alone in daylight . . . etc. But here we have our classic 'prototype for everything' all bundled up in one. And how about the modelling possibilities of a Bulleid on fire?!! Or one that's been on fire - an excellent use for one of those old Kitmaster models you couldn't motorise satisfactorily (but don't actually set fire to it, you don't want to die from toxic fumes!) More importantly, melting it would damage the structural integrity of the shape, so you'll have to

The former SECR lines' goods traffic was almost exclusively handled by the Maunsell moguls and the Wainwright C class 0-6-0s. Both are now available from Bachmann, enabling the modeller to accurately portray Eastern Division goods work. This splendid display was recorded in 1941 on the old SER line from Redhill at Ash Jct, on the long-gone Tongham chord to the LSWR's Alton line near Farnham. E C Griffiths

achieve the look by clever weathering).

These night freights go some way to explaining why there is little evidence of Southern freight in photographic collections: back in steam days film wasn't too good at recording images in the dark. This is also why the sniping at Bulleid for claiming his Pacifics were mixed traffic is a trifle unfair: since they were in use on passenger trains in the day, their night-time freight work was seldom recorded. Further examples: in 1961 the 01.20 to Yeovil Jct and 02.06 to Barnstaple Jct, both from Exmouth Jct in the middle of the night, were rostered to Light Pacifics, and the 04.04 to Axminster had an N15. The 21.10 and 22.00 from Nine Elms were regularly headed by Merchant Navies. All were freights. I've never seen a photo of any of them, nor any records of the locomotives working them.

The freights which usually *were* photographed were the pick-up goods trains. These spent much of the daylight hours hopping from one station yard to the next whilst trying to stay out of the way of the passenger trains. In this they were virtually the same as could be found on any railway in the country. They would collect the full wagons from the local yards whilst dropping off more full ones with deliveries (the railways tried wherever possible to back-load vans in particular), taking them to or from the local marshalling yards. Branch pick-up goods trains would do the same, being attached to the main line pick ups at the junction. Marshalling sidings would be placed strategically along the main lines to enable the pick up traffic to be marshalled into the longer main line freights; these would in turn be remarshalled at important junctions or strategic yards to

be sent on their way in other main line freights. Another example (one I was familiar with): the LSWR main line to Bournemouth was fed by overnight freights from the Western via Salisbury, Basingstoke, Nine Elms Goods depot and Feltham hump yard, amongst others. These would be remarshalled at Eastleigh and then again at Brockenhurst. Traffic for the Lymington branch would be sorted here as would the local traffic. Wagons for the "Old Road" via Ringwood would form another train, traffic for stations beyond Bournemouth would also go that way to avoid the congestion in the Bournemouth area and a pick-up goods would be prepared for the local yards at Sway, New Milton, Hinton Admiral, Christchurch and Boscombe, running to Bournemouth Goods. The same would happen in the opposite direction.

At the other end of the above 'chain' was London. The Western Section's principal London receiving depot was Nine Elms, which had to handle all the incoming perishable goods from the market farmers across the south and south-west. This then had then to be distributed to the shops, bakers, stores and open-air markets around the city in time for the early morning shoppers, especially in an age when fridges and freezers at home were only for the rich. Consumers in our period had to buy most of their produce on the day, so it always had to be fresh. Going out-of-period slightly, it was appropriate that Nine Elms locomotive depot was used to create the New Covent Garden Market, as the Nine Elms goods depot on the other side of the tracks, (which was also to be incorporated in the new complex) had been serving those self-same traders for a century or more before then.

Each of the Southern constituents had its own London goods receiving depots. The LSWR contributed Nine Elms, the LBSCR had one adjacent to an SER one at

Bricklayers Arms (which the Southern sensibly amalgamated in 1932) and the original LCDR had one at Blackfriars, where the produce of much of the 'Garden of England' was unloaded. Nearby, and actually *under* the railway itself, was the famous Borough Market, which gave its name to what was possibly the most congested railway junction of all. These goods depots (they weren't 'freight' depots!) were also the loading point for the produce of London businesses and the products of the Empire and other trading nations which came ashore in the great Docklands to the north of the river which was the lifeblood of the city. Each had landing stages on the river itself - it wasn't just a coincidence that the early railways sited their London termini near the Thames - and there were railway lines across or beneath it to connect to the other railway companies which principally served the country north of the river (in other words, the 'Frozen North' which, as all good Southerners know, starts just beyond Watford). In steam days those cross-river lines were really freight lines and the few passenger services operated over them usually failed to pay and had short lives. The concept of 'Thameslink' and 'Crossrail' are modern, in Southern days if you wanted to travel beyond the great termini you went 'down the Drain' or used the Underground system.

Those cross-river lines also served goods depots owned by the northerners: the LMS had a depot at Falcon Lane near Clapham and Knight's Hill near Tulse Hill, the GWR had South Lambeth and the LNER Brockley Lane at Nunhead. These lines brought locomotives and trains from the northern lines onto Southern metals (most of these link lines were jointly owned) and also took Southern ones in the opposite direction. So Panniers, J50s and Jinties were quite normal on Southern lines here. For the modeller the

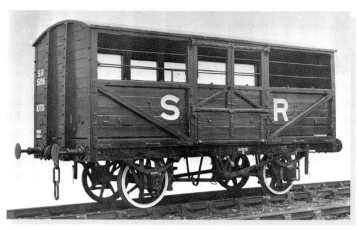

Whilst horses were treated to special 'boxes' cattle were carried in, well, cattle trucks. This one just has hand brakes.   *RCHS/Spence Collection*

possibilities are endless: there were many smaller goods depots squashed in amongst the blackened South London commercial premises such as Arfur Daley's and Del Trotter's lockups which can provide inspiration.

Special goods traffic was heavy. The Southampton area had a lot of it, notably banana traffic from the Docks to Nine Elms. This was as important as passenger traffic with fully-fitted vans running at quite a rapid pace, working amongst the passenger traffic. By the nature of shipping, much traffic was short-notice and intense: the arrival of a laden cargo vessel at Southampton could generate any number of special services, to almost any part of the country. A considerable proportion would require vans, which often had to be garnered from every possible location, the Southern frequently having too few available from its own resources and having to indent for the shortfall from other Regions. These would arrive "as required" as empty stock at almost any hour. In the late 1950s and early 1960s a form of 'mineral' traffic developed very quickly from the Fawley Oil refinery and the Southern received its only allocation of 10-coupled freight locomotives in the form of some 9Fs specifically for this traffic. Prior to that all manner of

steam locomotives were tried from H16 tanks through Ws and BR Standard class 3 tanks - just proving once again that the Southern wasn't set up for this kind of freight, and thus, from a modelling point of view, is even more fascinating. Another freight flow in the area was that of coal traffic from South Wales, which brought Western 8-coupled tanks to Eastleigh on occasion!

The Central Division had as much local and receiving goods traffic as anywhere and was characterised by the number of freight tank engines in use right into the 1960s. Due to its comparatively short runs and early main line electrification the LBSCR lines had a large number of freight tanks as no freight electrics were produced until the War. Had that not happened the Bulleid/Raworth electrics would have been multiplied and a great deal of Southern freight would have been electrically worked. The Eastern Division had one of the most numerous Southern freight locomotive classes in the 105 C class 0-6-0s and the principal Southern goods tank design for London transfer traffic was the W class which was, of course, part of the SECR locomotive tradition.

In Kent the electrification of the main lines in the 1950s brought an unusual - and unique in the British Isles - feature to some larger goods yards. This was because it was deemed unsafe to put live rails in goods yards but there was a requirement for the new electric E5000 locomotives to work freight trains. The solution was to fit a form of trolley-type overhead system in the yards only and the E5000s with pantographs. This had worked well on the Central Section with the Bulleid/Raworth electrics and was repeated on the Kent lines. It didn't last long but was a fascinating oddity. The Continental traffic led to many unusual wagons appearing, many being British loading gauge versions of foreign stock: these were trans-shipped by Channel ferries with rail tracks embedded in their decks. Again, short-notice traffic had to be accommodated and all traffic could be affected by events overseas or, as the famous headline had it, when the Continent became isolated due to fog in the Channel!

Another Brighton locomotive is seen on the Midhurst line at Petworth on 21 December 1960. The LBSCR had no long lines and found that tank engines could serve most of its needs. No. 32557 is a member of one of the most numerous 'Radial Tank' classes, the E4s, principally designed for passenger work but as frequently used on goods work. In Southern days some worked as far away as Sheerness and even, brierfly, on the Isle of Wight.

RCTS CH00816

The Kent coal field was something of an anomaly: don't imagine it as a little bit of Northern England transplanted to the Garden of England. It wasn't even discovered until the 1890s and wasn't very big. There were only four successful pits, Tilmanstone, Snowdown, Chislet and Betteshanger. Chislet supplied coal to BR camp at Nationalisation, only the KESR working for any time under BR, and the Kentish branches such as the Hawkhurst branch on which the annual hop harvest led to special freight trains as well as the celebrated Hop-pickers specials. These lines and individual Southern wagons will come under scrutiny another time.

Awaiting the road between Millbrook and Southampton Central is a Permanent Way train from the Redbridge depot. At the back is a 'Queen Mary' brake van, one of the first series, built on an ex-Brighton Elevated Electric power car chassis. It is branded 'Redbridge Works' to which someone has helpfully added 'RED' in chalk. What work requires so few supplies? A single 'Grampus' wagon carries a small load of ballast and the first bolster wagon has a few sleepers whilst the other one has two lengths of rail. A short bolster wagon at the front allows a degree of overhang of the latter. All-in-all, an eminently reproducible Engineers' train for the modeller! A Molyneaux/Noodle Books

and closed in 1969 after the BR End of Steam. The others closed in the 1980s, but it was their opening dates that are interesting, 1906, 1908, 1914 and 1924. Their heyday was thus almost purely Southern. However, the coal failed to sell to the export market so traffic was mainly towards London although there was an important local short-haul working to provide coal to the Dover Harbour tugs and lighters and the town's gasworks whilst there were also complete trainloads to the Bank of England's money-making plant - sorry, banknote printing works - at Overton on the Basingstoke to Salisbury part of the West of England main line. The Southern also had some special high security vans for this and bullion traffic. The discovery of coal led to an addition to the famous Col. Stephens Light Railway empire, the East Kent Light Railway being built to exploit the anticipated market. This brings to mind the Col. Stephens lines that fell into the Southern

Tailpiece: a brand new 'Pillbox' brake van is resplendent in its pre-war Southern paint scheme. This is one of the lighter-weight 15 ton vans: the majority were 25 tonners. Howard Butler

7 Infrastructure

A railway consists of many things, not just trains, although that is where most modellers' interests lie. Just as important are the things most of us lump together as 'scenery' and a number of modellers have made their names as specialists in building models or, rather, models of buildings and other ancilliary railway infrastructure.

Space, as ever, precludes more than a cursory look at the infrastructure of the Southern so here I'm just going to point out certain characteristic Southern structures and equipment. If the demand is there perhaps we'll be able to revisit the subject and give it the detailed attention it deserves.

Trains need stations and goods depots to ply their trades. These date back to the very beginnings of the railways when horses were often the motive power and

RCHS/Spence Collection

the animals continued to provide the means to haul railway road transport. The famous 'Scammell' units were known as 'mechanical horses': many railway terms date back to those days, the 'iron horses' were housed in 'sheds', like their equine predecessors.

Each railway company developed its own architectural style and, since there were many of them and many styles for each company, few railway structures were similar to one another. Generally, similar styles would be seen on individual lines (see the Bournemouth Direct feature in the form of 'Swaynton' at the end of this book) but the Southern drew much of these together by imposing standards for smaller items such as station nameboards, paint schemes, lamp posts and signalling.

Southampton Central's new buildings on the south side of the station were set to be the ultimate expression of its modern and forward-thinking image when built in 1934-5. Sadly, the little blip in the sky, a barrage balloon, wasn't sufficient protection from German bombers and it was blasted on the night of 20 November 1940 and then the new buildings were completely destroyed on 22 July 1941. RCHS/Spence Collection

Perhaps the best-known Southern 'house style' was its so-called 'Odeon' look which it used on all things constructed from the 1920s onwards. Concrete was the material of the age and the Southern put its inherited concrete works at Exmouth Junction to good use, churning out masses of concrete items ranging from platform edgings to lighting towers, lineside staff huts, fencing panels, nameboards, signal posts and footbridges to complete stations and signal boxes. Southampton Western Docks was the Southern's biggest project through the 1920s and 30s and the art

The modern brick-built but 'Odeon' style signalbox at South Croydon makes a statement by contrast with its Victorian predecessor. RCHS/Spence Collection

deco style of the 'Odeon' era was seen to perfection in the many concrete structures that turned the mudflats behind Southampton West (Central after reconstruction) into one of the most prestigious docks of all, the railway boasting that Southampton Docks were the 'Gateway to the World'.

The Southern didn't just use concrete, although the few lines it did build were very much the product of the material. A line to Chessington was built in the 1930s, electrified at the outset and all its stations were concrete, as were the stations on the Fawley branch in Hampshire, built on the opposite side of the River Test to the great Docks complex. It would later become best known for the oil traffic to the Esso refinery at Fawley, the station there eventually becoming subsumed in the sprawling mass of oil production.

Melding such diverse heritage into a coherent whole was quite a task. The Southern's Publicity department at Waterloo was blessed with a team of visionaries who increased the public awareness of the railway and what it was doing with a series of publicity coups which have stood the test of time. Simply naming the newly electrified suburban system as the 'Southern Electric' changed perceptions from that of an old fashioned steam railway to a cutting-edge transport system for the modern office worker meant that the term the 'sparks effect' entered the language and new communities spread like wildfire along the Southern edge of the Capital, all served by the Southern Railway.

Southampton Western Docks as completed in the 1930s. Included in the works was the World's largest dry dock, suitable for the massive liners such as the 'Queen Mary' that were the epitome of between-the-wars luxury travel. Naturally the Docks were a prime target for the German bombers and much reconstruction was necessary after the War, but the age of the car and the aeroplane would render much of this complex redundant. Southampton Docks were reborn once again in the age of containerisation and this area is still a place where motor cars are stored, but today they are mostly imported here. RCHS/Spence Collection

Both: Paul Hersey

The 'concrete' image was part of this publicity, the whole being a well-orchestrated campaign to reverse the negative image of the railways engendered by the Great War and the industrial strife of the 1920s, followed by the Great Depression. A good Southern model will feature concrete and publicity - British Railways continued the trend with colourful posters in the 1950s and 60s- which add immeasurably to a model's atmosphere and are as relevant as an engine shed or train of wagons snaking through the scenery.

The Southern inherited a great deal of infrastructure, including some magnificent examples of great Victorian engineering; this river viaduct on the Oxted line was built by the LBSCR. Not a particularly large or important structure, but built in sympathy with its surroundings, it typifies how the railway had become part of the country which it served. Smaller viaducts such as this are perfect prototypes for model railways and a reminder that even the South of England isn't flat, so baseboards shouldn't be either! A Fairburn tank passes above. David Chalmers

Railway infrastructure cannot be even touched upon in these few pages: the publisher's regular magazine for the Southern enthusiast 'The Southern Way' has many inspiring articles covering all sorts of aspects of the company and is highly recommended. It is essential reading for all modellers. I, too, will visit individual aspects in greater depth in a future volume of 'Modelling the Southern'. Meanwhile, here are a few illustrations of the immense variety of the subject to inspire you.   *All pictures: RCHS/Spence Collection*

Two sides of Clapham Junction in 1958, the LBSCR West London platform and the LSWR up main to Waterloo. The locomotive is the first of Urie's H15 'Chonkers', progenitor of the great British 4-6-0. Note the elevated signalbox.

Taking water at Three Bridges. The length of the arm of the water crane needed to reach the D1 is just one aspect to note: the Southern colour light signals, the station lamps, a can of oil(?) in the foreground, stop boards for the electrics . . .

Southern inheritance in the form of infrastructure precedes our look at the locomotives the company inherited from companies such as the SER, which built Godstone station

with its splendid iron footbridge and staggered platforms and the LBSCR which equipped little Rowfant with a handsome signalbox and level crossing gates which don't seem to cross anything. All will be revealed in the course of time!

8 Locomotive Inheritance

TheSouthern inherited a hotchpotch of locomotive types from its constituents, many of which survived throughout the Southern's independent existence and became part of the national railway fleet due to, firstly, the Southern's priority of electrification and, secondly, the long delay to that programme as a result of the Second World War and the paucity of investment money thereafter.

For the modeller, if not the operating authorities, all this makes the Southern an absolute gold mine of fascinating prototypes crying out to be modelled, but giving him the quandary of 'which ones will be correct for me?'.

A few of these 'inherited' locomotives are available ready to run, so the following should help modellers decide which of these are suitable for his period. Reference to such models doesn't necessarily mean

that I actually recommend them - I haven't bought or built them all, this is just for information! As before prototypes which are available as kits will be the subject of future books in this series.

Only locomotives which are available ready to run in 4mm scale are discussed here.

Beattie Class 298 2-4-0WT Standard Well Tanks
(available in 4mm scale from Kernow Model Centre)

The oldest were the 3 celebrated Well Tanks, built in 1874/5, designed by Joseph Beattie and tinkered with by his son William George, which had been retained to work the Bodmin & Wadebridge line to Wenfordbridge. As received by the Southern they had already been rebuilt twice, the second time as recently as 1921/2, looking somewhat different to their final form as they had stovepipe chimneys, wooden buffer beams and

All three of the long-lived Beattie Well Tanks are seen at Eastleigh shortly after withdrawal from their 'home' at Wadebridge. The one nearest the camera is the 'odd man out', no. 30856, with 'square' splashers to Beattie Junior's design. This one was cut up but the other pair were preserved and still run today.   *A Molyneaux/Noodle Collection*

prominent donkey pumps. They were rebuilt again in 1931-6 to the form we are familiar with, as produced by Dapol for Kernow. In this form, painted plain black, they worked until 1962, always at Wadebridge.

These were the epitome of LSWR duplication and renumbering! They were built as nos. 298 (thus the class designation), 314 and 329, duplicated in 1898-1901, to E0298 etc in 1923, to 3298 etc in 1935/1/6 respectively and finally to 30585-7 from1948. (By the way, the replacement LSWR no. 298 was a C8, scrapped in 1938!).

Their limited sphere of operation was widened occasionally, particularly on passenger trains to Padstow. They would also be seen on their travels, light engine or with rods down, to Eastleigh for overhauls. Twice they were seen east of Salisbury, on excursions. But there will no doubt be many more of these on the model railway layouts of the future!

Adams Class 02 0-4-4 tanks (Available in 4mm scale from Kernow)

Perhaps the best-known Adams class after the 'Radials', the smaller 02 0-4-4 tanks were introduced in 1889. They were the only LSWR locomotives to be built specifically for branch line duties (although Nine Elms always had a few) and were to perform that task well into the 1950s. There was just one variant, the final 10 having 6" taller cabs.

All 60 (nos. (30)177-236) fell into Southern hands in 1923 but were facing early withdrawal as electrification was releasing T1s and M7s for use in the country. However, the Isle of Wight railway companies contributed a motley selection of vintage locomotives to the new grouped company which saw that the redundant 02 design would be ideal for modernising the off-shore fleet. Accordingly, 23 of the 02s were shipped over between 1923 and 1949, eventually becoming the only class of locomotive working on the Island. These engines were all of the standard, lower-cab version, and were fitted with air brakes and, from 1932, extended

An O2 (the O is a letter, not a zero) is surrounded by M7s at Eastleigh, an eminently modellable scene as both classes are available in 4mm scale. No. 30193 sports a Drummond pattern dome: it isn't a true Drummond dome, being much wider than the real ones - compare it to the M7's dome behind. This was one of the last 'mainland' O2s, some of the Island ones also had these boilers for a while but they were inferior to the original Adams boilers and sent back to the mainland!

A Molyneaux/Noodle Collection

bunkers. They were re-numbered W14-36 on arrival on the Island (these being totally unrelated to their original numbers or date of arrival), and, from 1928, given names of towns and villages on the Island.

The principal variation in the appearance of both Island and mainland O2s was the fitting of Drummond style boilers to some engines. Two were genuine Drummond 1906 boilers but the other eleven had a rather fatter dome than the traditional Drummond design: these, an Eastleigh 1926 design, were universally disliked.

which weren't allocated p/p stock, such as the Padstow to Bodmin trains. Notable was 30200, which worked around Wadebridge with the Beattie Well Tanks in its last years.

All the O2s wore full Southern Railway passenger green livery followed by most of the Bulleid variations, a number on the Isle of Wight being fully decked out in the post-war malachite green, some with 'Southern' and others 'British Railways' spelt out. Once the final BR liveries were established they all sported the lined black

O2 no. W31 'Chale' stands in the Freshwater branch platform at Newport station in the early 1950s, a line which closed in 1953. The locomotive displays its Westinghouse pump on the side of the smokebox and an air reservoir on the tank: these are not for pull-push work but are for braking, the Island having all air-braked stock from pre-grouping days - a long time ahead of the mainland! Two Island O2s had p/p gear fitted, to work the Ventnor West branch, which closed at the same time as the Freshwater line. The Island O2s also had extended bunkers. Things might have been very different here if the proposed Solent Tunnel of the Edwardian era had been completed, with the Freshwater line being the main line on the Island rather than a backwater. Note the train indicator boards and the plethora of milk churns effectively clogging up the platform: even a little backwater carried many gallons of milk.

5 mainland O2s were fitted with air-control for pull-push duties from 1932, the year in which withdrawals commenced. However, only 8 had gone before the War, by which time Nine Elms, Eastleigh, Basingstoke, Dorchester, Yeovil, Exmouth Jct, Plymouth and Wadebridge had members of the class. Their duties included station pilot turns, shunting, and local goods work. A few were used on local passenger services

mixed traffic livery, with both early or late crests. The Kernow model will allow the modeller to have either mainland or Island versions, the latter no doubt giving rise to an explosion in Island-based layouts! All that will then be needed will be a range of ex-LBSCR and SECR coaches as modified to run on the Island: Bachmann have already announced plans to produce a PMV utility van as used thereon.

Drummond Class M7 0-4-4 passenger tanks (available in 4mm scale from Hornby)

The very first true Drummond engine was the first (no. (30)242) of an order for 25 suburban passenger tanks, replacing a cancelled order for more Adams class T1s and placed into service in February 1897. These were the first of the Drummond 'standards', using the short-firebox and 5' 7" drivers and were the famous M7s, a further 80 being added between 1897 and 1911. (Curiously, the last M7, no. 481, was the 16th-from-last Drummond locomotive built, in December 1911). There were numerous minor differences between batches and one major one, the final 40 having a longer front 'platform'. Slightly less obvious was the positioning of the front sandboxes, either above the footplate (incorporated into the splashers) or below it. Engines built at Eastleigh were initially classed as X14 but were later subsumed within the M7 class.

Although built primarily for suburban work, some M7s always worked at the larger 'country' sheds on secondary passenger duties right from their introduction. With one exception they all passed into Southern ownership as built. The exception was no.126 which had been rebuilt with a superheater by Urie and looked very modern compared to the rest. It only lasted until 1937 as it was front-heavy so was dismantled and its components used for spares. (If one takes the frames as the real 'soul' of a locomotive, no. 126 was renumbered 254, which was one of the short-frame series, although it now became long-framed, in standard form).

Some had been fitted with the LSWR variety of pull-push (p/p) control gear (a system of wires and pulleys carried over the carriage roof) but from 1930 this was replaced by the LBSCR type of air control, which was fitted to 31 of the long-framed M7s in that year.

30057 heads west along the 'Old Road' at Lymington Junction with a p-p train consisting of a pair of ex-LSWR 'Ironclad' coaches. There was a myriad of pull-push sets, most being elderly main line stock downgraded for these local duties and fitted with a remote driving cab. The M7 is one of the long-framed variety fitted with the Brighton pattern of air-control equipment allocated to Bournemouth for services over this line and the Lymington and Swanage branches in the 1950s and well into the 1960s. Bournemouth usually had around about a dozen of the class and none of the LMS or Standard classes were sent to Bournemouth until 1963.

David Chalmers

Some pull-push trains consisted of just a single control trailer coach, eminently reproducible on a model. The complicated pipework has been done for the modeller by Hornby on its M7 models. Here no. 30047 has no tail-lamp in position as it propels its single ex-SECR coach (either no. 3474 or 5) at Selham on the Pulborough to Midhurst line in 1950.
E C Griffiths

Electrification had meant that many of the class were redundant on suburban duties so this was a new lease of life and they soon started to be seen, albeit occasionally, on the other Sections. No. 55 worked at Maidstone for a few months in 1930, and in 1934 2 went to Stewarts Lane for Eastern Section work at Strood, Swanley, Westerham and Gravesend West. The London based ones worked most of the outer-suburban services to places such as Alton and Haslemere. Gradually, Exmouth Junction's allocation grew, at the expense of the 02s and T1s. In 1937 a further 5 engines were motor-fitted, the 36 such engines being spread between Guildford, Eastleigh, Fratton, Bournemouth and Exmouth Junction.

From 1939 to 1946 the smoke box wingplates attached to those M7s with below-footplate sandboxes were gradually removed, making a surprising difference to their appearance. All 104 locomotives survived the War and were transferred to National ownership in 1948, although no.672 fell down the liftshaft to 'The Drain' at Waterloo in June and was broken up there. The Southern had started repainting a few (3!) into full malachite green livery with 'Southern' on the tanks and then 4 had the same treatment but with 'British Railways' spelt out (Salisbury's no.(30)243 had both varieties). The whole class thereafter became BR mixed traffic lined black engines.

BR spread them around even more than the Southern Railway, sending 4 to the Central Division for use on the Brighton, Guildford and Midhurst trains from Hailsham in 1949, by which time Exmouth Junction had 25 of the class. Some of these soon went back east as BR Standard class 3 and ex-LMS class 2 2-6-2 tanks supplanted them and some of the displaced M7s went to Eastern Division sheds such as Faversham during the 1953 flood crisis. Brighton was also to become home to these engines after the crisis was over, and others went to Reading and Redhill for a short time at the end of 1953. 10 of the class were transferred to Three Bridges and Tunbridge Wells West in 1955 for the East Grinstead and Oxted line motor trains, all but one staying for less than a year.

Withdrawals started in June 1957 although they weren't completed until 1964! During that time four more M7s gained p/p gear, two also changing from short to long frame engines (see 126 above). These included 30031, modelled by Hornby as a p/p engine: the 'real' 30031 was a short-framer until January 1961 when it got the frames and p/p gear from 30106. Even in 1963 M7s were allocated to Bournemouth (14), Feltham (2), Salisbury (3) and Tunbridge Wells West (5). The last to go was 30053 at Bournemouth, the shed hosting M7s for use on the 'Old Road', the Swanage and Lymington branches until a mass withdrawal in May 1964.

These engines are a 'must' for almost any Southern layout: thank goodness, or, rather, thank Hornby for the provision of super-detailed models of the class in almost every one of its variations, no.126 excluded.

PS. Like all Southern engines, the M7s were frequently used on goods services and even as shunters . . .

Drummond Class 700 goods 0-6-0 (available as a limited run from 00Works)

The 700s were the second of Drummond's 'standard' classes to appear, all 30 being built by Dübs & Co of Glasgow in one production run of 30 locomotives in 1897. They also used the short firebox and had 5' 1"

The LSWR didn't have many full-time goods engines, but the 700s were the nearest to that type although they did head the occasional passenger train. M7s often helped them out! (30108, Hornby's only 'weathered' M7, is seen shunting at Poole on 11 June 60). Until the 700s were superheated they shared boilers with the M7s. In later years the 700s were popular for use as snow-plough engines, their last workings being in this role, after they were officially withdrawn. No. 30368 is seen close to, but not connected to, a snowplough at Eastleigh in the early 1960s. The latter would make an interesting model feature.
Above: RCTS CH00547   Below: David Chalmers

drivers. Their standard 6-wheel tenders had a 13' wheelbase. As they weren't a Nine Elms product they didn't have an alpha-numeric classification but were colloquially known as 'Black Motors' although they were green in LSWR days. Still, they were black under the Southern! Briefly, from 12/36 to 10/37 they were reclassified 'C', but that was most ill-advised as there were over 100 C class 0-6-0s already - the Wainwright SECR ones. The Drummond standardisation is seen to its fullest extent in this class: its somewhat odd wheelbase of 7' 6" + 9' 0" is the M7 driving wheelbase plus the C8/K10 driving wheelbase: the position of the driven axle is exactly the same for all these locomotives.

When the Southern inherited them they were in the process of a thorough rebuilding programme by Urie which involved the raising of the boiler centre-line and the fitting of superheaters, a process which was complete by 1929 and made them no longer standard with the other classes. By this time they were

secondary goods engines as the Urie H15s and S15s had taken over the heavy work; however, there was still plenty for the newly reinvigorated 700s, they even took their turns, in the best tradition, on passenger trains in daylight hours.

In 1925-6 20 of the class gave up their 13' wheelbase tenders in exchange for 14' ones to enable 10 T9s and the D15s to work on the Eastern Section. They did occasionally appear on Central Section metals on Sunday excursions to the Sussex resorts but were Western Section machines all their lives. This didn't preclude them making appearances on trains of Meldon ballast in connection with stabilising works at between Sevenoaks and Hildenborough in 1938 and then also on the Chatham main line around that town in preparation for the outer-suburban electrification scheme of 1939.

During the War Nine Elms had 20 of the class to work inter-company trains to the GWR, LMS and LNER via a circuitous route which couldn't accept heavy

Bournemouth's long-term resident 700 was 30695, which is seen passing the entrance to the coal yard at Boscombe on 26 February 1958. The engine has lamps rather than headcode discs in the usual Bournemouth line positions: at night lamps were used instead of discs, although this seems to be broad daylight!. The advertisement hoardings in the background are examples of lineside features seen in an unusual position, being angled to ensnare passengers on the station to the left of the photographer. Behind the engine is a furniture removals company's warehouse, containers of household goods would be unloaded from the kick-back siding here. Such traffic was a staple of Southern goods work. The tracks in the foreground lead into Boscombe's surprisingly well-ordered 7 road goods yard. This was a late addition to the railways of the area, opening within the station in 1897 and effectively becoming an overflow yard for the very near Bournemouth Central Goods Yard. In the 1960s Boscombe yard became a coal concentration depot, but it only lasted into the early 1970s. RCTS JAY2531

locomotives. This took them via Staines, Greenford, Calvert, Bletchley, Sandy and Cambridge, all of which they visited. All 30 soldiered on through the War into Nationalisation, which affected their looks but little. They were still black, but now with smoke box number plates and BR markings. At this time they were spread amongst Nine Elms (5), Feltham (8), Guildford (4), Eastleigh (3), Basingstoke (2), Bournemouth (3) and Salisbury (5). The latter used them on both passenger and goods turns on the S&DJR that ran from that city to Bournemouth via Downton.

In August 1957 30688 met a somewhat violent end buried in the end of an electric unit at Staines, but no more went until 1959, 11 seeing in 1962, the year in which I saw a 'T9' shunting at Wimborne which, on closer inspection, proved to have 6 coupled wheels. After that the 700s became my favourite locomotives of all. Following withdrawal in December1962 a number were reprieved in order to work through the heavy snowstorms of that winter. This meant that 30697 was able to work its last train (taking a Bulleid Pacific to

Works) on the day I became eligible to drive a car . . . but I'm not saying when that was!

No r-t-r models of these charismatic engines have yet been made by the big boys, but I live in hope. It is included here as, 00Works did produce a limited r-t-r edition, and I, naturally, bought one, which I numbered 30695, a Bournemouth regular. 30697 was a Guildford machine.

Drummond Classes T9 express passenger 4-4-0
(available in 4mm scale from Hornby)

16 months after the first M7 started work the first of 10 of Drummond's express passenger version of his 'standard' designs appeared. These were the C8s (nos 290-99), which were almost M7s with a front bogie and 6' 7" drivers and, of course, a tender. They had the same short firebox, but the next production run, of 30 engines, was built by Dübs & Co (like the 700s) and had a 12" longer firebox in an otherwise-similar boiler. At the same time 20 of this modified design were built at

T9 no.122 is seen approaching Nursling station in Southern days with a fairly substantial goods train of around 40 wagons. With reasonable gradients and few heavy minerals to carry, even large wheeled 4-4-0s could be useful freight engines. Many of the open wagons are sheeted, a feature which is infrequently modelled. The order of the wagons is also of interest: the various vans are spread along the train, indicating this is probably a pick-up goods.

Nine Elms, under order numbers G9 and K9. These appeared (with random numbers as replacements for earlier engines) between January 1899 and February 1900 and soon showed they were a vast improvement over the C8s. Dübs & Co built a singleton, no. 773, for exhibition purposes (it won them a medal at the Glasgow Trade Fair in 1901), which the LSWR purchased. A final 15 were built from December 1900 to October 1901, and were to give the class its final name, as the first of this batch were built to order no. T9. The 'Greyhounds' were unleashed!

By Grouping the T9s all had the famous Drummond 'Watercart' 8-wheel tenders with inside axle boxes and were being updated by Urie with the addition of superheaters, a process which Maunsell was happy to continue. The whole class of 66 engines was so fitted by September 1928 (no. 718); 26 of them ran in

Southern livery in their saturated form. The C8s weren't superheated and were withdrawn between 1933 and 1938, no doubt providing 10 spares of every kind except for frames for the rest of the 'standard' locomotives.

The T9s were so good that some were transferred to the Eastern and Central Sections to help out, following a three-way trial against SECR F1s and Brighton B1s and B2Xs The T9s won and the 'Gladstones' - the B1s - and B2Xs were condemned. The F1s (and SECR B1s) would go to the Central Section and the T9s to the Eastern. For these duties they received 6-wheel tenders, the first 10, all from the 'real' T9 group (with wider cabs and splashers) being fitted with 13' wheelbase ones from 700s to let them fit the short Eastern Section turntables, in 1925. They were allocated to Battersea and worked the lines to

Wide-cab T9 30307 shows off its ex-700 13' wheelbase 6 wheel tender, fitted when it was sent to the Eastern Section in early Southern days. Here, in 1952, it's working on former SER metals in BR days at Farnborough North, in the heart of the Surrey military area. The grass-grown platform in the background once resounded to the march of military regiments being entrained for action on the Continent: military traffic was (and still is) substantial on Southern lines. The guard's end of the SECR 8-compartment brake third no 3471 has yet to receive its 'S' suffix but appears to have been repainted into lined plain crimson livery. The engine also bears its LSWR power class H on the cab beneath the number, as modelled by Hornby on its first narrow-cab BR T9, no. 30724.   *E C Griffiths*

Sheerness, Dover and Margate via the old LCDR lines. For this work their tall capuchons, fitted when they were superheated, were halved in height, an alteration applied to the whole class before the War. On the Eastern Section they were treated as the equal of the Maunsell D1 and E1 rebuilds and shared duties with them. From 1933 they also worked to Eastbourne on the Central Section, to which a further 6 had been allocated in 1928, this time with 14' wheelbase 6-wheel tenders. Only one of these, 303, was a wide-cab T9. These worked trains from Brighton to Hastings, Tunbridge Wells, Redhill and Eastbourne although they usually worked along the coast to Portsmouth. After the electrification of the Brighton main line they were usually employed on the Mid-Sussex line via Horsham, 4 going to Battersea shed for this. They didn't appear on the Oxted lines until wartime once restrictions were lifted.

The 50 T9s remaining on their home metals still worked from most of the large sheds on cross-country and secondary main line trains. Just before War was declared 14 of them worked in the West Country, 6 at Exmouth Junction, 1 at Okehampton, 1 at Launceston, 12 at Wadebridge and 4 at Plymouth. Nine Elms had two, but one, no. 119, was especially repainted and 'bulled up' in 1935 to work a Royal Special to take King George V to Spithead for the Silver Jubilee Fleet Review. This engine would later receive Bulleid malachite green, successively with 'Southern' and then 'British Railways' on the tender and be kept for such special duties. It also retained a short capuchoned chimney at a time when all the others (with the notable exception of (30)721) were losing theirs.

During the War some T9s were allocated to the (higher-profile) S&DJR when the LMS recalled its 4Fs and 2Ps. Most of the Battersea engines returned to the Western Section, some replacing the U1s on the 'Withered Arm' where they had been 'unappreciated'. During the War they were often to be seen on local goods and pick-up duties, in the traditional Southern manner, following which 13 of the class were fitted with oil-burning equipment in 1947/8. Although successful in this form all were stored in September 1948 when the scheme collapsed suddenly.

Following that there were two bouts of 'Indian Summers' for the class, 8 returning to Battersea for the last time in 1948/49 and Nine Elms engines working a series of main line trains on the South Western mainline in 1950.

BR repainted a few in plain black before standardising on mixed traffic lined black, a scheme which suited them well. The green one, 30119, was, surprisingly, an early withdrawal in 1952, a year after the 13 oil-burners and 7 others were taken off the books. 30119 was one of 8 1952 withdrawals, at a time when most Drummond classes were being phased out. Surprisingly, only one more went, in 1954, before general withdrawals began in earnest in 1956.

Slowly they retreated, like the warriors of old, to the West. Eastleigh tended to find plenty of work for them, even after the dieselisation of 1957 onwards, and the 'Withered Arm' continued to need them despite a massive influx of massive Pacifics. At the beginning of 1959 there were still 3 at Nine Elms, 1 at Basingstoke, 6 at Eastleigh, 4 at Bournemouth, 2 at Salisbury and 7 at Exmouth Junction, but the Nine Elms ones went off to Exmouth Junction in the middle of the year.
The new decade saw 14 survivors split as to 6 at Eastleigh (most in store) and 8 at Exmouth Junction. Four of the Exmouth Junction engines went in early 1961 and by October there was just 30120 left. Someone besides me had a soft spot for these brilliant engines and The Nation wanted it as part of the National Collection.

So 30120 once again became LSWR no. 120 and was adorned in the rather bilious Urie green livery, a first for the engine in its final form as it wasn't superheated until 1927. Still, why should we worry? In this form it continued to work local trains from Eastleigh and surprised me at New Milton station by turning up on the morning local to Bournemouth before the transformation was general news. It spent two years in this form before being retired to Fratton for official preservation, again on my 17th birthday!

The 'Greyhounds' are a bit of a minefield for modellers, with their two forms of splashers and cabs, three types of tender and various smaller detail variations. However, Hornby have produced all the major variations (with the exception of the 13' tenders), both of splasher/cab and 6- or 8-wheel tender types and the various liveries. Notable amongst the latter are 30119 in BR malachite, complete with small capuchon and 120 in both its preserved faux-LSWR livery and 'correct' Maunsell olive green.

Urie Class N15 express passenger 4-6-0 (available in 4mm scale from Hornby)

Urie's second class of 4-6-0 appeared after the end of the Great War and was to prove to be his greatest legacy to the Southern. The 20 engines of class N15 (nos. (30)736-55) were the progenitors of the Maunsell 'King Arthur' class and were little different in appearance. The principal visual items were the stovepipe chimneys they had from new, the smoke box doors (chimneys and smoke box doors were replaced by Maunsell items in the 1920s) and the shape of the steam-pipes above the running plate. The cabs were the same as fitted to the 'Eastleigh Arthurs' and the tenders were the first of the standard Urie 5,000 gallon pattern.

Besides showing an N15 on a goods (at Salisbury) this shows the rear of the tender of 30748 'Vivien' which bears evidence of her time as an oilburner in 1947. Those engines so altered were fitted with electric lighting together with tubular Bulleid Pacific style tender ladders: don't simply re-number a Hornby Urie N15! The ones to avoid are nos. 30740/5/8/9/52, the latter also boasting a Lemaître multiple blast pipe and wide chimney. The Stones turbo-generator for the electricity can just be seen behind the smoke deflector. A Molyneaux/Noodle Collection

The N15s received names associated with the Arthurian legend from 1925 and were assimilated within the 'King Arthur' class, the designation N15 also being applied to the whole class. Their liveries and duties were also the same, the cab profile restricting them to the Western Section. Bulleid fitted 5 of the class (nos. (30) 736/7/41/52/55) with Lemaître multiple blast pipes and wide chimneys. 3 of these (nos. (30)737/52/55) had their smoke deflectors modified to the vertical position but the other two didn't. (30)755 proved to be exceptionally fleet of foot and was placed in the Nine Elms 'Lord Nelson' link.

During WW2 they were principally used on goods trains and 10 of them went to the LNER for such duties from late 1942 for 8 months. All survived into BR ownership, 5 of them at that time being briefly fitted with oil-burning equipment, by which time they were mainly allocated to Nine Elms, Bournemouth and Eastleigh sheds, with one at Feltham for the heavy overnight West of England goods. Withdrawal started in 1953 and finished in 1958 with 30738, the last survivor, working from Basingstoke shed on the Waterloo stoppers. The following year their names were re-used on the Southern's BR class 5s.

Hornby's N15/'King Arthur' models include some of the more useful variations between the many iterations of these 4-6-0s and a number of the Uries have appeared, including one of the engines fitted with the wide chimney, as 30737 'King Uther', appropriately 'King Arthur's' father.

Wainwright class C goods 0-6-0 (available in 4mm scale from Bachmann).

The first, and possibly *the* iconic, Wainwright/Surtees design, especially after Bachmann included it in their 2011/12 programme. 109 were built and all reached Grouping although one had undergone drastic changes. To get it over with, it was no. (31)685, which was rebuilt as the sole member of class S as a saddle tank and used as the Bricklayers Arms yard shunter from its conversion in 1917 until its replacement by a diesel shunter in 1951. It was then tried out at Hastings (briefly) and finally used at Dover as shed pilot, being withdrawn in September 1951.

Simple, rugged and powerful, the rest of the class had long careers as the main goods locomotives in use on the Eastern Section/Division of the Southern, with no visible changes to their profile other than the fitting of 7" shorter chimneys early in their careers. They were used on passenger trains (of course!), the annual hop-pickers specials often featuring the class right up to their demise. Whilst they were allocated to Eastern Section sheds they did stray to the other Sections, notably to Portsmouth with naval specials in 1925, to Southampton with spoil trains in the early 1930s when the Western Docks were being constructed, and on excursions. During WW2 1229 and 1585 reached Weymouth with Dunkirk evacuation trains and 1508 and 1717 double-headed southbound through Winchester. No.1716 worked the 'Night Ferry' on 7th January 1939

Artfully framed by the trees C class no. 1225 is seen at the head of a goods working which has a high proportion on coal wagons as it approaches Kingsley Halt in 1947, just 10 years before its closure. The Halt was the only intermediate stopping point on the Bentley to Bordon branch, where the Southern met the northern extension of the Longmoor Military Railway. Wainwright Cs were not often to be seen on ex-LSWR metals at this time so this was a noteworthy working. It had probably worked through from Guildford. E C Griffiths

after an LN failed and in 1949 31717 (again) assisted a Light Pacific on the 'Thanet Belle'.

Only 2 missed being BR engines, nos. 1262 and 1499 being withdrawn just days before BR took over the remaining 106 engines. The changes that organisation brought about saw the Cs being downgraded to less exacting tasks with 9 members of the class being shedded at Guildford (which had always seen them working on the ex-SER line from Redhill to Reading) to replace the LSWR Adams class 0395s. Members of the class were often used to clear the juice rails of snow and ice in the winters of the 1950s. However, the Kent Coast Electrification saw many of them withdrawn and a few transferred to the Western Division at Feltham and Nine Elms where they worked for a short while. The class became extinct in 1963, except for two which escaped into Service stock as DS239/40 (ex 31592/272) the first of these being saved on the Bluebell Railway in 1967.

Even the Wainwright Goods livery was elaborate but they were in a grey livery when they became Southern property and received the normal progression of Southern liveries until becoming plain black under BR.

Before the Bachmann models were announced, the C was released by 00Works as one of their limited edition ready-to-run models. Bachmann will no doubt produce the only variations that these engines displayed in real life, ie., the chimneys.

Perhaps the best-known passenger workings of the Cs are the hop-pickers specials, many of which ran onto the Hawkhurst branch. This is 31588 leaving Paddock Wood with a train for Hawkhurst. David Chalmers

Stroudley Class A1/A1X 0-6-0 tanks (available in 4mm scale from Hornby).

These are the famous 'Terriers', the small 6-coupled tanks that Stroudley produced for the London area inner suburban routes from 1872. Their history is amazingly complex, as the LBSCR had 50 of them, nos. (326)35 to 84, which had become outclassed on their suburban services by the turn of the century.

Many were sold and many withdrawn by the Brighton, but the Southern inherited no less than 24 of them, from all of its principal constituents except the Isle of Wight Railway. 5 were working on the Island in 1923, one was owned by the Newhaven Harbour Company until 1927, and one each came from the LSWR and SECR. Thus the Brighton supplied 16, 14 of which had been rebuilt with extended smoke boxes and longer boilers and reclassified A1X, as had two of the Island engines. The SECR, LSWR and one Island one (an ex-LSWR one) had non-standard boilers but were all rebuilt to A1X specification by the Southern by 1936. The Southern Railway only retired 9 of the class during its existence and one more was added to stock in 1948 when the Kent & East Sussex Light Railway was nationalised, so

BR inherited 15. During the War the KESR had hired 3 members of the class at various times.

The Isle of Wight allocations varied over the years: one of the inherited ones was scrapped and 3 more were sent over in 1926-9. 4 were returned to the mainland in 1936, 2 being withdrawn and 1 joining the majority of the class at Fratton, which was responsible for the Hayling Island branch services, giving it an allocation of 8 'Terriers'. The 4th one went to Lancing as a works shunter. In 1937 the mainland locomotives were distributed between Fratton and Newhaven and the two Works. The other 3 were in Service stock, two at

*The famous 'Terriers' are well known for their exploits on the Hayling Island branch into the 1960s where they were normally seen being dwarfed by enormous passenger coaches including the celebrated 'plastic' BR suburban proto-type built at Eastleigh with a fibreglass body, S1000S. Rather less well known are their exploits at Newhaven where 32326 is seen shunting a few wagons at the Town station on 24 November 1962. The Newhaven Harbour Company had once owned a member of the class (**top**) but it was sold to the Southern.* RCTS CH01971

Lancing and one at Brighton Works. The latter upon withdrawal in 1946 was restored as LBSCR no. 82 'Boxhill'. The other of Lancing's two was the former SECR one which had received an A1X boiler in 1937 but retained its A1 smokebox. It too would be preserved, as no. 54 'Waddon' and shipped to Canada in 1963.

During the War, in 1942, pioneer no. 2635 worked at the Shell depot at Hamble and as shed pilot at Bournemouth; 2661 was lent to the War Department at Gosport. In 1949, after Nationalisation, Ashford had 4 for KESR work (3 later going to St. Leonards), Fratton 6, Newhaven 2 and the Works 3. 32662 worked an RTCS special on the Lyme Regis branch in 1953. When the KESR lost its passenger services in 1954 the 'Terriers' continued in use until replaced by diesels in 1958, often also working a van train to Bexhill West. After Fratton closed in 1959 the remaining 'Terriers' were transferred to Eastleigh shed but still used on the Hayling Island line until its closure in September 1963.

The Capital stock 'Terriers', being passenger engines, wore Southern green livery, the Newhaven and Works ones black. However, after the Brighton Works A1 was restored in 1946/7 to Stroudley 'improved engine green' livery (yellow) there was sufficient paint left over for its replacement to be finished in the same livery. This was 2635, which became 377s, (DS377 to BR), and was to retain the Stroudley colours with the legend 'Brighton Works' on its tanks until its withdrawal in March 1963, having been returned to general stock in 1959 as 32365. Sadly, although it was the first of the class, it wasn't preserved. All the rest of the service stock engines received BR lined black and the last were withdrawn in 1963.

The Dapol 'Terrier', later released by Hornby, has been issued in many liveries but without the variations exhibited by the prototypes. It is almost a 'must' for a Southern layout, and most modellers find excuses to run them far from their prototypical locations! After Fratton closed in 1959 the remaining 'Terriers' were transferred to Eastleigh shed but still used on the Hayling Island line until its closure in September 1963.

In the next volume I will be describing 'Locomotives built for the Southern', these being the many BR Standards and LMS classes built to cover the shortfall in motive power that took place after the War.

If inspiration is still needed, how about this magnificent pair of pictures of the iconic Hayling Island line? **Here** *32650 arrives at the eminently-modellable Hayling Island terminus in 1954 whilst, on the* **previous page**, *another 'Terrier' scuttles across the flimsy Langstone Bridge a year later. OK, the bridge might be a little difficult to reproduce, but perhaps a diorama with an expanse of water in the foreground and a bridge in the background is feasible. It most certainly is an inspirational scene!*
Both: E C Griffiths

9 Modelling Inspiration
a personal perspective

Some people, quite rightly, might ask who and what am I to be pontificating in this manner upon things Southern? I will give you my biography to let you make up your own minds and understand what has inspired me. This is going to be the most personal part of the book, where I will show you some of them.

Parts of my background have appeared in brief snippets throughout this book but it all started almost a year before Nationalisation in a nursing home close to the western end of Bournemouth West station. Frozen in place for that hard winter my parents first drifted to a small flat in my maternal Grandmother's former B&B in Brockenhurst before moving to New Milton when I was about 18 months old. My first memory is of being frightened by the whistle of a Bulleid Pacific (it might have been something else - I was in a pram!) near Hinton Admiral, thus securing my connections with the Bournemouth Direct line forever.

As an infant I recall being taken to New Milton station to watch the trains, especially when my Father caught a morning train at around 8.30 in the morning to go to work in Bournemouth. Once I saw one of the Diesel prototypes there, possibly on that train. School holidays would see me ensconced on the station platforms at New Milton with a flask and sandwiches but no money, so I couldn't escape on a train. Still, I had a good, if solitary, time there. Occasionally my Mother would bring my younger brother along and we'd picnic on the station, but this put him off trains rather than encouraged him. He liked guns.

My Father recalled his days commuting into London from Hadley Wood station in London and I remember a happy holiday with his sister in Potters Bar when my cousin would take me across the golf course to watch the trains on the ECML. A4s impressed me no end (and still do, Bulleid was involved!).

My first model railway was a Rovex Princess set. My Father quickly got bored with it and built a larger oval layout using some Graham Farish fibre-based flexible track, also buying me a GF Black 5 and a Prairie tank. After he had mysteriously spent many days and evenings in the loft he took me up there one day and showed me a splendid new model railway layout which went around half of the loft, which he described as 'mine'. We spent many happy hours up there and the locomotive fleet increased rapidly. One particular purchase was a Triang L1 4-4-0 which I wish I had kept.

Christmases and birthdays were easy for my parents: a pile of red Triang boxes and their contents would keep me happy every time. One model I always hankered after was a Graham Farish Merchant Navy, but it was beyond our means. I've recalled my experience aged 9 at a friend's birthday party which started my fascination with the real ones in their rebuilt state.

Another abiding memory is trips to Lymington on the pull-push trains with M7s and visits to the Isle of Wight. The coaches were a mix of crimson and green liveries. Holidays were spent in a flat in Swanage owned by one of my Father's friends and Saturdays were spent at the station watching Bulleids on the Waterloo through trains. My cousins still lived in Brockenhurst so visits to them included long periods standing on the 'Black Bridge' (it was painted green) across the country end of the station. Thus I saw Bulleids, T9s, M7s and everything in between including the beautiful Brighton Atlantics on the through train from that town. Visits to London were always undertaken by train, where I was somewhat disappointed by the (to me as a child) soulless electric units.

In the early 1960s girls, Beatles and alcohol took precedence over the by-then run-down railways and a move of house saw the end of my loft layout (although it may still be there for all I know). When steam came to an end in 1968 so did my railway interest as I tried to build a career in accountancy. However, the series of articles by 'A Model Railway Study Group' expounding the virtues of real scale modelling standards, known as P4 were to rekindle the interest.

Having been stung by taunts of 'playing with toy trains' I had given up modelling but this seemed an altogether higher calling, akin to art, and I was hooked once again. I could now boast that I wasn't playing with them but creating true replicas. And it worked: my friends accepted my new interest and some even wanted to see the models! Visits to Studiolith Limited in Oxford were fascinating but frustrating as many of the much heralded scale items were in short supply in those early days. Then during the 1970s the Protofour movement started to gather pace and Area Groups were encouraged. One day I was contacted by Paul Marchese with a view to arranging a meeting with other local P4 modellers to form such a Group. About half a dozen of us met at his house and agreed to form such a Group, initially concentrating our efforts on his P4 layout of Sidmouth.

My interests had now turned to the LSWR period, specifically July 1922 (I was getting a little anal by this time!) and I set about building an accurate model of a G6 using a Wills kit. I quickly found out this wasn't possible and combined parts from an O2 with the G6 to produce a fair representation, mounted on a scratch-built 3-point compensated chassis. An O2 followed and I was quite proud of its haulage capacity on a fully compensated chassis.

Pressures within the P4 'fraternity' turned to fratricide and one of our Group meetings was attended by some of the rebels from the North London Group who were setting up a rival Scalefour Society. Rival presentations were made to us by them and the original P4 movers but we decided to go with the S4 crowd, who had put forward some even more accurate standards than the P4 ones. I acquired a set of S4 gauges and tried to upgrade my existing P4 track, without success. By this time I was in my own house and had use of the spare room in which I was building a terminus station based on an extension of the Corkscrew to Bridport. It had extremely elaborate pointwork!

The Group now turned its attentions to building a group layout, following the new enthusiasm of the Scalefour launch. We met in Martin Welch's flat to discuss what to do. Some of us were Southern enthusiasts and some, notably Peter Squibb, GW enthusiasts. Ne'er the twain could meet, except that there was one station locally where they did, and it was close by: Winchester Chesil. With just a copy of an old Trains Illustrated article showing it at closure we resolved to build an exhibition quality layout exactly to scale to help launch the new Scalefour Group. But how could we get plans and accurate information about it? It was decided to reconvene a week later but in the meantime advertise for information in the Hampshire Chronicle. We got an immediate reply and at the following week's meeting we welcomed one Kevin Robertson to our fold. He was writing the definitive work on the DNS line and had all the information and plans we'd ever need!

We were all young and penniless but I was working for a firm of accountants who had a maker of kitchen units as a client. They were in the process of relaunching their range of units with metric measurements and had a surplus of the old Imperial larder cupboard sides which I could have free of charge. Thus the model of Chesil started on 6' 6" boards, an error we soon came to regret.

My task was to build the trackwork with Paul and, as I had the Scalefour gauges, I suggested we should build the layout to the new, accurate standards. I constructed the pointwork by the signalbox, the first I had done with such absolute accuracy. We attended number of Scaleforums with our models and built up a good relationship. One of our members was the charismatic

Mike Jolly and he knew how to build anything - to perfection. He constructed all the buildings for Chesil as well as some rolling stock.

Progress was quite slow on Chesil and I was not there to see it finished, due to a move away to the West Country at the beginning of the 1980s. Then my interests turned towards historical railway films. Finding I couldn't access them, a bout of illness resulted in my being confined to bed with a new-fangled video recorder and the desire to watch railway films on video. Again, I couldn't find any. Upon recovering I resolved to find some films and to transfer them to video myself. This project then morphed into a project to film railways and I created a business to sell these called Railscene, which was to incorporate archive film with newly filmed material on a regular basis, magazine style.

That kept me occupied for a quarter of a century or so, during which time Kevin Robertson and Mike Jolly became involved. We had an office in the old railway yard at Romsey station and I tried to turn it from the 'real thing' to my first love, modelling. We were at bit ahead of the game with 'Railscale', the modelling equivalent of Railscene, as cameras and lights were pretty unwieldy in the 1980s. We filmed the construction of a large N gauge 'project layout', built by Mike Jolly and visited a number of famous layouts to include in the programme. One famous occasion took place at Pendon, where our hot video lights melted one of their beautiful models: a GWR B-set! If you see a B-set at Pendon today, it's not the original one . . .

The railway video market has seen many changes and I have concentrated on programme commissions for many years as the modern scene has lost its lustre for me. I am just nostalgic for the 'good old days', especially those of my youth. Nowadays it is the 1950s that fascinate me the most. Getting old and in need of a new challenge a chance meeting with Kevin at a local show resulted in his suggesting that I write a book called 'Modelling the Southern' and this has been the result. Originally intended to be one small volume, the research has thrown up so much in the way of material that even two may not use it all. Kevin has generously agreed to let me 'spread' it so if you as a reader have anything you might like to see or feel I have ignored, left out or simply got wrong, you are invited to let me know through Kevin at Noodle Books.

I do hope you've enjoyed this first effort. As I said at the beginning, all errors are mine alone. Please forgive me them, but please tell me what they are!

I shall leave you now with a series of views of model railways which I have found particularly inspirational or which have some connection with my own interests and memories. You'll know which means what to me from the foregoing!

Modelling inspiration
Newhampton

In this chapter I want to show you some of the Southern models that have inspired me over the years. In my P4/S4 days I was also a member of the South Western Circle and was often inspired by the locomotive models that were displayed at various meetings of the Circle.

I also enjoyed the outings of the models by members of the Southampton Model Railway Society, whom I met in the early days when they were based at Sholing station. These photos of their model 'Newhampton' could only be based on Southampton Terminus!

Here we see comings and goings from the terminus at Newhampton. The real Southampton Terminus was the original terminus of the London and Southampton Railway which opened throughout on 11 May 1840 from its Nine Elms terminus in London, both termini being designed by the great Sir William Tite in the Italianate style. The model's backscene reflects the architecture of Southampton and the engine shed is modelled on the standard design of the LSWR at the beginning of the 20th Century, which was built in many configurations but always in the same style.

The models reflect Southern ownership in the mid 1930s, locomotives and stock bearing Maunsell

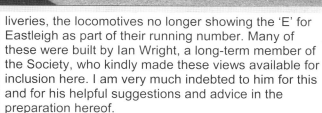

liveries, the locomotives no longer showing the 'E' for Eastleigh as part of their running number. Many of these were built by Ian Wright, a long-term member of the Society, who kindly made these views available for inclusion here. I am very much indebted to him for this and for his helpful suggestions and advice in the preparation hereof.

On this page we are out in the countryside approaching Winterbourne Junction. The signalbox is a classic South Western structure, dating back to Victorian days. The earliest LSWR signalboxes had very elaborate valances and were quite tall and upright. (A late-surviving example was to be seen at Southampton Tunnel Junction until its closure as part of the Bournemouth Electrification). The model here is of an LSWR Type 1 box, dating from the 1860s when signalling was very young. Other examples lasted right into the electric era. The signalman is waiting to hand over the branch token, very much as happened on the main line at Winchester Junction for Mid-Hants line trains.

Maunsell Moguls are in great evidence on this line: on the right a U1 with a short train of Ironclad stock passes under a typical two arch bridge and past two of the lattice post lower-quadrant signals. The characteristic inset sides to the guard's and luggage compartment identifies the coach, whose general lines were followed by Maunsell when he introduced his first range of standard Southern coaches with the lower windows from 1926.

Further along the U1 passes an N on another train of LSWR stock, this time wooden bodied and fully panelled. All this coaching stock was scratch built and hand painted. To our right a Maunsell 'Eastleigh Arthur' with its Drummond Watercart tender streaks out of the tunnel before passing the Newhampton Yard signalbox and the sidings at the north end of the station complex. The corrugated lineside hut makes a change from the usual concrete hut, but more about the latter later!

A fine line-up of ex LSWR locomotives stands outside Newhampton locomotive shed. Prominent in the centre is Adams 'Jubilee' or A12 class 0-4-2 tender engine, many of which were still in service in the 1930s although withdrawal was quite rapidly thinning the ranks. The real no. 643 nearly made it to becoming BR stock but was with-drawn in July 1947.

To the right is the back end of another Adams locomotive, class T1 no. 16 being a member of what can be said to be the larger version of the O2s and this is then seen passing the tall station signalbox as it leaves with a local passenger service. The T1s were withdrawn at the same time as the A12s, their tender counterparts.

Behind the 'Jubilee' is a member of the iconic LSWR T9 class of 4-4-0s, another scratchbuilt example built many years before Hornby launched theirs.

Behind the T9 stands the 'Eastleigh Arthur' seen opposite, now turned and revealed as 'Sir Launcelot', King Arthur's Champion - and his wife's lover!

In the background is a montage of local scenes, setting this railway very much in Southern Hampshire.

Two final shots of this inspirational layout: in the **top** view the U1 leaves the terminus and passes the goods yard as a Urie-modified 700 prepares a goods train in the yard behind and then, **below**, is seen approaching Winterbourne Jct with a clear road on the main line.

A corner of the Scalefour Winchester Chesil layout in the production of which I was involved at the early stages. Many fine modellers joined after I left, including Martin Finney who went on to design some splendid etched locomotive kits of (ugh!) Great Western prototypes to use on Chesil as well as one or two Southern ones. Martyn Welch also dropped out early on and went West, but only after building the seminal Hursley in 7mm scale (he showed us his first 7mm wagons at one of our earliest S4 Group meetings). The model of Winchester Chesil was eventually sold to the Hampshire County Museum Service.

Today Chesil resides in the recreated GWR station building at the 'Milestones' museum centre in Basingstoke but there are very few photographs of it. I took this view of the loco shed corner - the building here was made by Paul Garnsworthy - at the time the main part of the layout had been covered by a board to display a Lego exhibition! Sacrilege, but Chesil would soon be returned to *public scrutiny*

Modelling inspiration
Romsey

Perhaps one of the best-known models of the Southern was the Southampton MRS' layout depicting the station at Romsey, on the Eastleigh to Salisbury line, which followed the Newhampton layout. The original line was one of two from Eastleigh (or Bishopstoke as it was), the other going to Gosport, which made the London and Southampton Railway change its name to the London and South Western Railway when they opened. A later line diverged to the south of Romsey station to reach Southampton via Redbridge and the Southampton and Dorchester Railway (the original S&D) resulting in Romsey having a junction at its south end. The Redbridge line was built as part of the so-called 'Sprat & Winkle Line' from Kimbridge Junction to Andover, where it connected with the Midland & South Western Junction Railway, later part of the GWR. Romsey was a cross-roads in railway terms, seeing a substantial goods interchange traffic from two Great Western lines, at Salisbury and Andover Junction. GW locomotives thus ran alongside Southern ones at this fascinating location - and I had an office in the old goods yard!

Modelling inspiration
Fisherton Sarum

Graham Muspratt (Muz) has become something of a Southern legend in recent times for his portrayal of the Southern as it turned into the Southern Region of British Railways. This was a poorly represented era in modelling circles until Muz opened our eyes to the possibilities, not only by way of a myriad of liveries, but foreign locomotives, the 'Leader' and many older classes at the ends of their lives rubbing shoulders with the new fangled Bulleids. I think it's best for me to let him explain the concepts, models and background for himself . . . *(but, like Arnie said 'I'll be back!' - in vol 2)*

H15 number 519 is an unusual visitor to the shed and is turned whilst an N1 on a rake of dia 1774 40T stone hoppers heads west to Meldon on the main line behind the shed. Another unusual visit lurks behind in the shape of Maunsell 350hp diesel No 1 built in 1937.

The purpose of this layout/diorama was an interim measure to provide a showcase for some of my rolling stock, as I was not in a position due to space constraints to build either of the two other layouts that I have ambitions for. I model the Southern Railway between 1946 and the very start of nationalisation into 1949.

Having a large and varied collection of locomotives I felt a simple (did I really think it would be simple!) way to display these was via the construction of a motive power depot type layout/diorama. Having looked at the plans for various Southern sheds such as Salisbury and Bricklayers Arms it was soon realised that a compromise was needed. In the end I used Salisbury as the inspiration for the layout (as it has a family connection) and the basis for the structures on the layout.

The name originates from the fact I wanted to retain the link to Salisbury without actually calling it Salisbury. The current station at Salisbury, to differentiate it from Salisbury Milford (later closed to passengers and kept solely for goods traffic) was originally called Salisbury Fisherton as it is located on Fisherton Street, with the original pre 1901 shed called Fisherton shed. Old Sarum, of course, is the famous hill fort and Roman centre forming part of the origin of Salisbury.

The key elements taken from Salisbury were as follows:

Coal Stage and ramp,

Turntable positioning relative to coal stage and water tower building,

Substantial water tower building with stores and engineman dormitories below,

LSWR design style of shed albeit reduced from ten roads to four,

The slightly elevated running lines and carriage siding at the rear of the scene.

The shed itself has been transposed to the east and is accessed by a kick back arrangement rather than a fan of sidings to balance the space utilised and enables baseboards of 3ft depth to be utilised.

The up and down running lines at the rear of the layout allow main line trains to pass the shed in the background and gives the opportunity for some of my other rolling stock to be seen.

N1 Class No 1822 trundles west with a rake of dia 1774 40T ballast hoppers heading for Meldon. The N1 has been converted from a Bachmann N class with a rebuilt front end and modified cylinders and valve gear whilst the hoppers are much modified Lima models.

Above: *The Southern-style water cranes (scratch built from brass tube, rod etc) frame T1 class number 10, one of Salisbury's pilot engines shunting wagons on the coal stage ramp.*
Left: *A view from the shed roof over a busy yard as a number of classes of locomotives including: Merchant Navy, N15, N, Lord Nelson , Light Pacific and Q1 are being prepared or awaiting their next duty. The turntable and imposing water tank and stores building can be seen to the rear.*
Below: *School children chat as the postman deliverers to the freelance cottage scene behind the shed's imposing water tower and stores building.*

All photos: courtesy of Chris Nevard and Hornby Magazine

Modelling inspiration

Swaynton for Milcliffe-on-Sea

It could be New Milton, Sway or Hinton Admiral, but it's Swaynton, and it's all three! Douglas Smith's magnificent model of the Bournemouth Direct doesn't need trains to show off its wonderful atmosphere: these views send me back half a century to the 'happiest days of my life'.

All photos : Philip Hall, courtesy Wild Swan Publications Ltd.

Swaynton doesn't just capture the spirit of the Bournemouth Direct, but the whole of the Bournemouth main line: the tunnels at each end represent the original London & Southampton Railway's line 'through the chalk' north of Winchester and an MN emerging therefrom is, well, just sublime! Hornby's replica MN brought my interest in model railways back to life in the Third Millennium.   *Both photos: Philip Hall, courtesy Wild Swan Publications Ltd.*

I'll end where I started, at New Milton station. This encapsulates all my memories and provides me with the inspiration that is part of the title of this book. These four photographs of New Milton were taken by Nigel Kendall, a guy I knew in my teenage years but didn't even know was a fellow railway enthusiast!

This is what I saw when I stood at the London end of the Up platform as the driver of a Rebuilt Bulleid Light Pacific looks back for the guard's 'Right away!' and whistle. Frequently the Pacific would slip madly: when I was very young and made train noises I thought they all went 'Chuff, chuff, chuff-chuff-chuff-chuff . . .'

New Milton was a product of the railway age. Between it and the crumbling cliffs at Barton-on-Sea was Old Milton, the village on the main road from Lymington along the coast to Christchurch and Bournemouth. I was born in Hampshire, raised in Hampshire, but where I was born is in Dorset. When I was young Dorset started at County Gates in Westbourne and the carriage sidings at Bournemouth West were half in Hampshire and half in Dorset. New Milton's focus was on Bournemouth and we usually travelled to the town by train, even when we had a car. My Grandmother still lived near the West station so I would stop there for a while before visiting her. The highlight of the day was the arrival and later departure of the 'Bournemouth Belle' so when Hornby brought out

their Rebuilt 'Merchant Navy' and 'Bournemouth Belle' models my Mother bought me them for my birthday. Four days later she passed away, so it is a rather special model to me in an infinite number of ways.

Overleaf there is a plan of New Milton and a 'Merchant', no. 35014 'Nederland Line' passing the neat little signal box at the Bournemouth end of the up platform. I recall one day being summoned from the balcony of this holy-of-holies by the signalman who gave me a shilling and asked me to go and buy him 'Fish and Six' for his lunch. I was very proud to do that for such an important figure and was rewarded with a short visit to watch him in action and the trains passing by.

The other photograph overleaf shows a Standard class 5 heading towards London. I didn't like these stark machines, particularly as they had replaced the lovely N15s (although 'King Arthurs' still appeared) and even took their names. Nostalgia is a great thing however, and I now look back at all the Standards with affection and will go into their stories and detail their activities on the Southern in the next instalment of this series.

All images of New Milton station on the next four pages courtesy of :

Nigel Kendall/Southern-Images.co.uk

NEW MILTON

SCALE

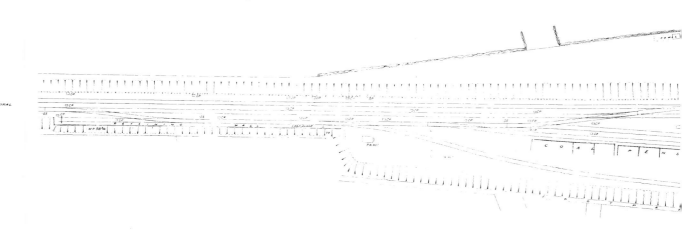

A final panorama of New Milton. From the western end of the goods yard a little footpath gave me a variety of views of the station and yard. Here another Standard, an Eastleigh class 4 Mogul, is engaged on the daily pick-up goods turn as a 'Spamcan' races through with a Bournemouth express. It was a fascinating place: it had rather more stopping trains than either Sway or Hinton Admiral and Douglas Smith has based his Swaynton timetable on New Milton's timetables for this reason.

In the right background is the principal feature of the little town in the mid 20th Century, its somewhat elaborate water tower. I always wanted to climb to the top to look down on the station but it was never to be.

Beneath it was a somewhat shanty-like collection of small shops and kiosks on Station Road, which in those days had shops on one side of the road and houses on the other. The shanties were a small sweet stall, a flower seller's, a taxi office and the local coal merchant's premises. The latter had his business in the goods yard and the coal staithes were always well filled. They can be seen in the middle distance in front of the corrugated iron goods shed, which boasted a canopy over the track feeding it and the end loading dock.

Sadly, the lovely pine trees which Douglas Smith has featured at Swayntion are long gone at New Milton,

although those at Sway still stand tall over the station there.

To the right front of the above view is one of the standard concrete huts of the Southern: a picture of a railway scene with one of these will always shout out 'Southern' whether there's a train in view or not. As a tailpiece, if you don't have one on your model you can't say you are truly 'Modelling the Southern'!

Acknowledgements

I should like to thank all those who have supplied me with photographs and information to help with the preparation of this book and the many authors of books and albums about Southern subjects upon which I have drawn freely (I now know how much effort you've all put into them!) and to those who have kept the interest in the Southern so alive for so long. Much information has been gleaned from various internet sources so thanks to those people as well. I can't name names as that would take up most of the book, but I trust I have acknowledged all the photographers as appropriate.

Finally, thanks to Kevin Robertson for the inspiration and the patience to see it through.